Teachings of the Immortals

So...
You want to live forever?

MIKAL NYGHT

Teachings of the Immortals

Publisher: Eye Scry Publications
www.eyescrypublications.com
copyright © 2010, 2013
All rights reserved
First Printing: February, 2010
Second Printing, Revised & Expanded Edition: 2013

ISBN 13: 978-0-9766897-7-5
ISBN 10: 0-9766897-7-4

WHOLESALE INFORMATION

For information about wholesale rates,
or to order additional copies, please email us at...

INFO@EYESCRYPUBLICATIONS.COM

VISIT THE AUTHOR'S WEBSITE
WWW.IMMORTALIS-ANIMUS.COM

Teachings of the Immortals

This is the voice of the vampyre twin
Whispering secrets of the dark evolution
From the place of silent knowing.

If you hold too tight
to your dayshine lives
the world might crumble
in your hands, quicksand.
Treat the clay as magick instead,
use it to make your vampyre twin
and don't be afraid to climb inside.

Introduction

Out of this World

WHERE IT ALL BEGAN

Teachings of the Immortals is a work that has been in progress for well over 19 years at the time of this second edition revision – March, 2013. What you will find in these pages are teachings which came to a group of us who were involved in Toltec sorcery, chaos magick, and the pursuit of personal immortality.

It was in 1994 when we first went to see *Interview With the Vampire*, which turned out to be a major catalyst in my life – awakening within me the awareness that I was a mortal being who was going to die if I didn't do something about it. But what to do? While I would love to tell you I went looking for Lestat and found him, that would be, unfortunately, a lie. What I did do was to open myself up to the realm of all possibility, asking myself the questions which are crucial to any spiritual journey. It begins with one simple question: "Who are you?"

It is impossible to describe the spiritual pain, angst, and longing I experienced as the deeper messages from *Interview With the Vampire* began to haunt me day and night. It wasn't an obsession with the movie or even the characters. It was an inescapable fixation on the darker truths hinted at within the film. In short, it forced me to question the very reality in which I lived – and it was through that questioning that I eventually came to see that the world is nothing like we've been taught to believe.

The Vampyre Within

Over the months that followed after seeing *Interview With the Vampire,* myself and two good friends began experimenting with any and all manner of magic – largely because there did not appear to exist any logical, straightforward manner of attempting to contact the immortal kingdom. None of us were strangers to ritual and the concepts of intent[1], manifestation and the

---

[1] Underlined words will be noted which may be further explored in the glossary at the back of the book. An explanatory text in itself, the glossary will expand your understanding and awareness Use it.

application of Will. I had been (indirectly but undeniably) a chaos magician all my life. And it wasn't long before we began to receive evidence that our cries in the dark did not go unheard. Believe what you will. Tell yourself this is all only a writer's fantasy if it will make you sleep better. But in the end, you probably wouldn't be reading this book if you didn't already have some similar story to share, some similar encounter with the unknown which changed your life forever. The simple truth is that we began to receive letters which seemingly appeared at random on the computer in my office.

Letters from a vampyre.

At first, the letters were largely playful and, yes, seductive. We were being courted, we were told. We were being tested. We were being considered as candidates for immortality – and yet, it was not as simple as the Hollywood depictions make it seem – not as simple as inviting a vampyre into one's bedroom and exchanging blood. The letters were not just seductions. They were *teachings* – outlining what can only be defined as a systematic undoing of the programs and belief systems which hold us prisoners to the consensual mortal world – the dayshine world as we have come to call it.

Over a period of several years, we were instructed via these letters, as well as through numerous Ouija board sessions and gnosis-trance-channelings. What we were being taught was essentially the process of self-willed evolution – the evolution from mortal to immortal, the transmogrification of human to other-than-human. What we were being guided to see was that it is our own mind which creates reality – but the hardest part is getting past the programming which tells us we are but impotent children in meat suits wandering aimlessly through the garden, at the whim of some god or goddess. The hardest part is giving ourselves permission to explore beyond the box, outside of the matrix, past the confines of Plato's cave.

What we were being taught, ultimately, was how to visualize, nurture, create, and manifest our own "double" – or, to use other terms, our vampyre twin, the immortal other, the higher self, the dreaming body. There are dozens of names for it throughout the various cultures, but it all comes down to one thing: we have within ourselves the ability to be anything we choose to be: including vampyre, immortal, eternal and infinite.

—

The hard part is knowing no one can do it for us. No, not even other immortals – although you will find as you progress on your journey that other immortals may serve as mentors, teachers, benefactors and even muses. It is a solitary journey of self-creation – but don't be discouraged. The good news is that it is a journey of wonder, imagination, creation and manifestation. Nothing is taken away from the mystique and allure of the vampyre – in fact, that allure and mystique becomes all the more potent when we realize and allow ourselves to accept that the thing we desire most can be real... if we are willing to go through the work to *make* it real.

WHERE TO START?
With yourself. That's what these teachings are really all about – undoing the programs which hold you in a mortal prison, and fully realizing your potential by embracing the infinite power of the creative force within you. Allow the impossible. Bring it forth. Demand it. Manifest it.

What does it look like? Who's to say? Perhaps your vampyre twin will be an exact doppelganger of how you appear in your own mirror. More likely, it will take the form of the thing you desire most – for this is how the muse is created and nurtured. This is how we trick ourselves into chasing the muse for as long as it takes to complete the task of this dark evolution. The twin may appear as anyone or anything, including animals – thus the legends and myths of vampyres being shape-shifters. That is the power of the twin. Maybe s/he will look like you. Maybe s/he will look like Tom Cruise or Angelina Jolie or Kathy Bates or a black cat or white wolf. It's your avatar – but it's far more than a passive icon. It is a quantifiable field of energy – the energy body – which you create, nurture and manifest as the vessel to house your awareness beyond the dayshine world. Remember: there are no limitations and no boundaries. Create it in the Now, and it exists throughout time – past, present and future. That's the power of quantum comprehension. We are powerful beings with the ability to recreate ourselves as anything we choose to be.

The only obstacle standing between you and your twin are the programs and belief systems which tell you it can't be done.

If some of The Teachings appear to be repetitious, it's because this is how we learn. You didn't grasp mathematics in a single lesson, nor will you assimilate the teachings in a single reading.

Be patient with yourself. Stop. Listen to your heart. Taste the wind. Feel the flame that fuels the search. Love the pain of the waiting.

If some of The Teachings appear to be brutal or hurtful, remember that the hardest battles we fight are with ourselves. Our greatest enemy is our own complacency, and our spiritual teachers have been charged with the task of keeping us on course... even when it may appear to be in direct opposition to what we *believe* we want at the time.

The only rules are to harm none – this includes both humans and animals. Evolution comes not from killing or harming, but from an utmost respect for life. A respect so profound it demands continuity in the form of immortality.

Thou art God: create yourself accordingly.

WHAT IS IMMORTALITY?
That's the question, isn't it? When I first began this journey, I thought of immortality as simply a continuity of my physical existence in some manner or another. I'm not talking about reincarnation or any other hokey religious mumbo jumbo. I simply believed that immortality was about living forever. And... it is. But it may or may not be in the way we first think – so another thing to remember on this journey is to keep a flexible perspective. Don't get married to the idea of physical immortality, for example, because the true and ultimate nature of immortality appears to be far more connected to a quantum state than an organic one. Put another way: the act of transmogrification may actually be seen as a migration of one's totality from an organic body into an energy body. This may or may not involve mortal death – there are many schools of thought on this, and none is any more valid or invalid than the others. You are the creator of reality – a phrase you will hear oft-repeated throughout the Teachings. Some may transcend death altogether while still in organic form, while others may choose (for a variety of reasons) to undergo the process of organic death as a means to release the spirit from its organic prison and free it to inhabit its inorganic energy body.

So what is immortality? This is a concept that will be explored indirectly throughout the teachings – the key being to maintain a fluid awareness, an open mind, and an open heart.

THE PURPOSE OF THE TEACHINGS

If we believe we already have all the answers, we can learn nothing. Part of the Teachings will challenge you to put aside your preconceived notions about literally everything. Whatever you think you know about vampyres or immortality, whatever you may believe about God or the devil, whatever you may think of the notion of reincarnation or the afterlife... let it go whenever you pick up this book, for the purpose of the Teachings is to free your mind from your pre-existing belief systems and social programs so that you may begin to think for yourself and truly start to *see* that most of what you believe about the world is not only untrue, but is propaganda put in place by the powers that be to hold you prisoner and slave to the consensus reality. As with the movie, *The Matrix*, we are often appalled to discover that our minds are not really our own – unless we take upon ourselves the task of freeing them.

That is what the vampyre does. And that is what the Teachings will enable you to begin, if you have not already done so. Ultimately, your own dark twin – your own immortal double/other – will take on the task of fine-tuning your immortal education (through whatever means you may decree: gnosis, channeling, Ouija, automatic writing)... and that's when it gets more interesting than you can possibly imagine. That is when the mortal self has successfully created the vampyre twin to such an extent that the twin begins to take on a life of its own... a life which will inevitably embrace and nurture the mortal self until the two are one, a dual spirit which takes on the characteristics of what may be called a singularity of consciousness.

WHAT IS A SINGULARITY OF CONSCIOUSNESS?

Put simply, it is the totality of oneself: mortal self, immortal other, and all the other manifestations/parallel-lives the immortal other has experienced. For those already at higher levels of practice, you sense and Know that the vampyre within you has walked this earth for centuries. Some might mistakenly call this evidence of past lives, but instead it is the parallel lives of the Dreaming body – the vampyre within who has lived countless other lives, not in some past realm of history, but within the infinite & eternal Now... within _you_.

When the mortal self eventually conjoins wholly with the immortal twin, the singularity of consciousness is the result: the all-inclusive total of both, which is greater than the sum of its parts.

You are becoming _yourself_ – the manifestation of your utmost potential. This is also what the Teachings will show you.

You are taking upon yourself the power and the ability and the responsibility to manifest the vampyre within – to Be the immortal spirit which has been whispering in your ear for longer than you can remember.

This is where The Teachings begin.

_____
The Vampyre's Apprentice
March 2013

Getting the Most from The Teachings

1. The teachings are presented as brief vignettes. *This is not a book you read from start to finish in a single night.* It is a grimoire of self-creation, intended to be contemplated slowly so as to be absorbed and assimilated wholly. For the most part, the teachings are written in heart-tongue – a language of spirit which bypasses the more logical/intellectual areas of the brain and speaks directly to the magical/spiritual components of Self. For that reason, it is imperative that the seeker open himself to Knowledge on an intuitive level, rather than merely trying to comprehend the words on an intellectual level. Listen with your heart. Hear with your Spirit. See with the third eye. Then you may Know.

The Teachings will be presented in two volumes. Book One will focus on some of the earlier teachings which appeared in letters as mentioned in the Introduction. Both books are crucial for a total understanding of The Teachings, but neither alone will make you a vampyre. Only you can do that. The Teachings can assist you in reaching a level of awareness where you have the ability to make a choice of such magnitude with awareness and responsibility for the consequences. *[Editor's note: While it was originally planned for The Teachings to be presented in two volumes, this seems unlikely at the time of this second edition revision. The author has made the decision to release segments of The Darker Teachings on his forum, where they may be discussed in an open and nurturing environment. Should a second book become an announcement will be made on **www.immortalis-animus.com**. –DV, 2013]*

2. The teachings are more suited to advance practitioners who may already have the foundational background of understanding that the world is nothing like we have been taught to believe. However, even newbies will benefit if they apply themselves with diligence, respect and, most of all, an open mind that has been freed from the programs & belief systems which are an automatic part of any human being on Planet Earth. If the mind has not yet been freed, these teachings may aid in the process. If the seeker truly does not wish to be freed, these teachings may result in severe emotional or spiritual distress.

Proceed at your own risk, with the knowledge that to be awakened from the illusion is not a metaphor or game. It is the most real thing you will ever do. And the most dangerous. There is no going back.

3. Take nothing at face value. These teachings were channeled into the mortal kingdom in a language and mood suited to the channeler, and to the students whom the immortal master was instructing at that time –

so at times there may appear to be personal comments which could appear vague or nebulous. But keep in mind – the act of becoming immortal is a process of self-willed creation – and part of that process is a seduction of the senses by one's own immortal other. It's not the words that are important. It's the message contained within the words – what lies between the lines as much as what is written on the lines themselves. Put simply: don't believe what you read here. Take it in. Suckle it. Nourish it. But by all means, test it for yourselves. Self-creation is not about following someone else. The Teachings are a guide and a grimoire. You are the magus.

4. It is recommended to use this book as an intuitive guide. Pick it up and turn to a page at random. Where your eyes come to rest on the page is your lesson for the day. You'll find it probably has relevance to events going on in your life or ideas you have already been contemplating. If you are on level of resonance with the vampyre kingdom, you will find this practice to be amazing and validating to your path. Truth seeks those who seek it. If you keep coming back to the same lessons over and over, look for patterns. Look for what you are hiding from yourself. Open your heart. Stop fighting yourself.

5. Quantum theory: all things exist within the realm of possibility, but only some things will be forced to go through the motions of actually occurring. This is a path of imagination, creation and manifestation. Buddha once said, "We are what we think." Everything begins with a thought but it cannot stop there.

6. The short poems you will find interspersed throughout are also teachings in themselves. Like Zen koan, they are meant to stimulate the mind and stir the imagination. Which way does time run – upstream or down?

7. Imagination, sexual stimulus, and sensual wondering are part of the process of evolution. So the vampyre speaks to our hearts and spirit as much as to our intellect. Ultimately, your twin an be anything you want it to be – because you are the god of your own creation. We create the twin (which may not be identical, but may be of opposite gender – which is most often the case!) to be not only our teacher and spirit guide, but to also be our dream lover and seducer – because we are multi-faceted beings who must use every tool at our disposal to lure ourselves into the immortal condition, within the night that never ends. If this sounds like a riddle, it isn't. It is the simple truth which lies beyond the world of illusion in which we find ourselves. As a child, you probably lay in bed at night and daydreamed and fantasized about all sorts of wondrous things.

This is the nature of creation – but unfortunately we lose sight of that power as we grow older and become assimilated into the consensus. The vampyre seduces us back to a purer state, back to a place within ourselves where we are free to dream. And if we embrace the potential of our own power, it gives us the ability to enter the dream and to literally *be* what we have the potential to be: immortal, eternal, infinite.

8. The teachings are not metaphors, although some may be presented in that fashion. You may ask, "Are vampyres real?" Yes – as real as anything can be. Remember: *You* are the creator of reality. Quantum science has proven that we are interactive with the creation of reality. If you want to learn more about that, try THE HOLOGRAPHIC UNIVERSE, THE TAO OF PHYSICS or THE DANCING WU-LI MASTERS. While it isn't necessary to have a quantum comprehension of the world, it can help in freeing your mind from its traditional belief systems.

If you want to be a vampyre, you can be a vampyre – the trick is having a firm grasp of what that really means. And like everything else in this world, *being* a vampyre is not what you have been taught to believe. The reality of it is actually far *more* than the usual myths. Vampyres are not the blood-sucking creatures portrayed by Hollywood. They are, in essence, custodians of Time, pure energy capable of manifesting as anything they may choose. Point being: if the traditional ideas/images of vampyres appeal to you... you can have that. *You can be that.* But don't limit your vision to *only* that. Don't be confined by the boundaries of old myths. You don't have to drink blood and you don't have to sleep in a coffin, and you don't have to shun the sun. Unless you want to, of course. The immortal condition gives you the power to choose who and what you will be, right down to a molecular level.

Thou art God. Create yourself accordingly.

Teachings of the Immortals

A Twisted Grimoire of Vampyre Transformation

I have given you the apple so you would be driven out of Eden out of your naked complacency. I do not attempt to show you fantasy worlds that do not exist but to reveal to you the illusory reality of the world in which you live.

-The Gnostic Vampyre

Be Advised...

The teachings are presented as brief vignettes, in no particular order of importance. _This is not a book you read from start to finish in a single night._ It is a grimoire of self-creation, intended to be contemplated slowly so as to be absorbed and assimilated wholly. Pick it up and turn to a page at random. Where your eyes come to rest on the page is your lesson for the day. Go no further until you have assimilated the lesson totally.

The teachings are seduction as much as instruction.

This is the Way of The Dark Evolution.

Who Are You?

Choose who you will be for eternity as if you are choosing who you will be for eternity. I know a lot of dissatisfied gods and disgruntled monsters, and even more bedraggled angels dragging their wings behind them with tears in hollow hallowed eyes for all the programs[2] and self-created limitations they carried with them from one world into the other, and it's as I've told you before: trying to untie the bonds on my side of the night is like a puppet cutting its strings only to realize it has nothing but strings on which to swing. This is why I am a vampyre, you see – for it is a only a word that allows me to be anything I might choose to be: angel or monster, friend of fiend, princeling or pirate or executioner or shepherd, and not one thread or shred of it hangs on the strings of what any other creature believes I should be, or even upon what I myself might once have believed when I made the decision to become this thing so that I might have the freedom to be ever-changing yet never straying from the identity of the singularity that is the seed and the seat of *I-Am* beyond all words and pseudo-human identities.

Confronting the Consensual Reality

What if I said you are already immortal? You are already a vampyre, a being of energy capable of incredible feats, and with the power to live forever? Stop. Listen to the response of your internal dialog. Does it argue with negatives? Does it tell you you're just a mortal fool? If so, this defines where your work must begin. Stopping the internal dialog is the first step to learning to hear the voice of the vampyre twin - the higher self, the dreaming self, the immortal self outside of time. What you may not realize is that there is a sinister force at work which may be viewed in terms of the social mind, the hive mind, the collective mind, or what some mystics have called the foreign installation. Whatever you call it, know this: it is the 'foreign' mind in that its sole function is to maintain the status quo of the

---

[2] Throughout these teachings, underlined words will be noted which may be further explored in the glossary at the back of the book. An explanatory text in itself, the glossary will expand your understanding and awareness Use it. [Yes this is a repeat footnote because we understand you probably didn't read the introduction.]

collective <u>consensus reality</u>. It is the Agent Smith operating in plain sight with your agreement and approval until such time as it is recognized and excised. This, too, is part of <u>The Work</u>. Ah, but for as long as you are governed by the social mind, you may not even believe The Work is a viable possibility.

Balance of Power

You have the power to create reality while I am only its servant. A word of advice: If you ask me to physically appear in corporeal form while making the invitation psychically, is not the risk then entirely mine - that I reveal myself and my powers to you just because you ask? Ask me to appear at the edge of a mineshaft or on a tall cliff, then *you* be standing at the precipice when I appear. Then the risks are equal. I'm not asking you to stand on the road and tempt real death, only to stand in the darkness and take a real chance with what you're asking. Quid pro quo. That is what it means.

Defining Death to Trap Him Within the Definition

Is death the natural end of the journey? Quantum science defines life well: corporeal existence manifested through cellular animation. The same science speaks of death: the cessation of cellular animation; a state of non-being; discorporation; presumed cessation of consciousness.

Even quantum science cannot address it properly, you see, for it is much harder to define a negative than a positive. We taste life even if bitter and filled with sorrow. Vampyres drink it and call it red wine. It is real. Death is a nonentity, and this you can only know with certainty after you have passed through it in one way or another. If there is a god, then god is death, but science says death is nothing, so I must therefore conclude that god is nothing if not nothing at all.

Undoubtedly you think I speak in riddles. Does this irritate the soft skin of your mind and make you long for the comfort of mundane-satin thoughts? I hope not, for if so I cannot save you. I would not want to. It is as I've said before: vampyres are the only true custodians of time and as such the only real keepers of the faith of Man. A contradiction, no? We are disconnected from Man and his religions yet the nature of us is the goal of every religion. We are immortal: god's promise to the faithful. Cry

---

blasphemy, sacrilege if you will, but *I am the only god I know*. If I create you it is for more than just a shallow lifetime. It is for <u>all</u> time.

The Essence of Vampyre Nature
This isn't a hunt that's meant to end when the hounds capture the fox. I, fox, could have stayed in the briars, but because the hounds caught the right scent, my red eyes peek out again. Chase me, I run. Catch me, I vanish. How does one hold the fox without first killing it? This is the essence of vampyre nature. Do you see it or no?

The Dilemma
The surface only reflects. Beneath, the waters are icy, filled with danger. Do you dare to dive? If the water isn't deep, the plunge might kill you. If you don't dive, you die anyway, an old woman at the edge of the sea. What to do?

Vampyreland is a state of mind
   (whole, chimera, paradox).
Mortals label it illusion
   to willfully delude themselves
   into believing magick is fallacy
   so their sanity stays safe and sane.
I drink their quantum veins 'til I'm drunk
   but they seldom see me.

Undoing the Dayshine World

What makes a vampyre's heart start to beat? None of us know but I believe it's anger, defiance, and fear: the insane need to defeat the reaper in his own bed at his own game of rape, the anger that transcends even the grave. If that's madness I want to be among the believers, you see. Will you join me? Do you have what it takes to defy the chosen God and gods of men? Can you go against that grain forever or is this a rebellious lark whose song will end before it begins?

If you learn nothing else from me, know this, for it is the secret to everafterlife:

> *When the blood turned to wine and the soul-deep cry of mystical belief became just a silly hymn to sing one day a week, when men hired prophets to see their visions and shamans to search for their souls and scribes to tell them what to believe and priests to feed them cookies and juice, when it became easier to settle for ritual and take a dip in a baptismal pond than steal a drink from the bleeding heartbeat of the immortal river's source or dare to swim in the pool of genes that will suck down those who don't believe, that was the day the brute got his scythe and man gave up his chance for real life. That was the day Magick died.*

I am the greatest proponent of religion because *I am the only god I know*. This isn't for the masses. You live in a world that says I'm unreal, but have you asked yourself who says so and why?

The consensus will damn those who make the search for the real thing real, they collaboratively curse you and me for pursuing this darker reality and they call it insanity because they've given up any chance of finding immortality, and they don't want eternal life to be real for others if not for themselves, so they create Death and make him more whole in <u>The Program</u> because it's simply, absolutely, without a doubt *easier* see? Better to believe in streets of gold and brimstone lakes and unseen cities in the sky than to believe they have the power to believe eternity real in any real sense of the word. They don't want my road because it's lined with snakes and eternally uphill and if they can't take a cab or a plane to immortality they'd rather pretend it's a fantasy

---

18

island that fell into the sea in the days when Atlantis was a suburb of Greece.

My prayer for your mortal Self:

> *This life is over, my love, so close your eyes for the last time and make a wish. There's a single candle on the cake and it burns brightest behind your eyes. See it? Do you know it's really your soul already gone to vampyre heaven? Now trust your intellect to take you the rest of the way and know it's an energy pure and whole unto itself, the flawless vehicle that will bring you home to eternal life. Yes, my baby. Close your eyes and we'll blow out the light together.*

Is this truth or riddle? Ah, that is the riddle.

Fairy's Tails & Dragon Scales

I don't believe there are any fairies or dragons or magickal beings left in your world because man has believed them away or locked them up in children's books. Every time we hear the words: That's just a fairy tale (or) There's no such thing as vampyres, whole worlds end, and if you're not careful you start believing it too. Ah, but what will happen when the world stops believing in you?

If it's all a lie, what is truth?

If everything in the web is a lie, how do you get outside to find the truth? If an entire reality is based on lies, is that reality not then entirely false? Ah, but the danger is this: live the lies long enough and they become true and then the <u>dayshine</u> world will own you and the shovel will turn down your bed too.

Seasons of the Vampyre

Feed me a reminder of mortality
   to bring me back to life,
   thick red tea (bitter please)
   brewed from fallen leaves
   found huddling next to a sepulcher.
The birds in bone bare trees are black
   and fly only at dusk, never singing,
   and mortals who pass through move swiftly,
   whistling superstitiously.
Sometimes late at night I hear the shovel whispering,
   turning down the bed.

Without apologies to the gravemaid, I go the other way. I'm a vampyre, and will never own real estate at Forest Lawn. I find the stench of death enlightening if not desirable. Most humans don't love these autumn winds but I am reminded again of what I am and what I can do when I put death to death. In fall lives the promise of grief if action isn't taken now, the reminder that winter will win, the knowledge that spring is nature recreating herself from a seed (not a thing of eternity), and summer is laziness that makes the soul complacent while calling it rest. Thoughts like these are not from me but residents of the wind.

Walk in it and they might get in your eyes, opening them wider.

The Fall

Standing on the wrong side of God doesn't come easy to those pampered by family or society, for even if it's not a question of theology it turns to matters of right and wrong and those are answers that live inside you and not in rule books written by philosophers and pious fools, and the one thing you must bring to the vampyre gene pool in addition to all else is the ability to answer these questions for yourself without cheating on the test.

I can tell you that everything you think you know is built on the perceptions of other men, but unless you step outside their world, you're bound to get tangled in the mess because they're the ones spinning the web in which you live unless and until you yourself take over the spinning. If you're born to be a vampyre, the left side of God is the only place you can be, see? But if you try to embrace the night when you're really a thing of the light, the <u>fall</u> will turn you wrongsideout and your world will collapse, a self-deceptive perception you never bothered to alter.

You can't live in a world you can't perceive and you'll die in the <u>fall</u> if you don't do what I'm telling you. If you don't have the underworld (vampyreland) firmly beneath you when we yank the rug out from under the world you've always known, where could you go but into the arms of the <u>brute with the scythe</u>? He has a keen interest you see, for he knows I'm the wily vampyre king who's pulled the wool over his eyes before.

What is the fall? Simply this... it is the dance between this world and the next, yet there is only one world in the end, divided only by perception. And it is in the fall that you'll feel the brute as hard as any lover you've ever known because he's as real as I am and just as seductive. He'll court you with flowers and a bed that's really a cold pine box. But if you let me hide you while he's inside you, he'll move on like the fickle prick he is, and I can slip your soul back into you with an injection of dreamflesh and vampyre blood, and you and I will tell the tale for ten thousand years to come.

These are only words of course. Symbols to entice mind, body and spirit... a seduction of the senses so that you will come to yourself and not the arms of the brute when you find yourself falling into the Fall. Sleep lightly now. I am with you always.

Vampyre Paradox

It is the time of year to taste the smoke from the fires in other peoples' chimneys, roaming streets wet with rain not yet fallen, wandering dirt roads still dusty in the storm, courting lightning under barren trees. Do you understand? Do you know what I am and what I'm going to do to you in the span of a heartbeat? This is how your world ends: not with death, but an awakening to your immortal awareness.

The Unnatural Nature of Death

We've talked of death before, but when his claws scrape close, the view is not distorted by the blinders placed over your eyes by cooperative agreement between society and the brute with the scythe to keep you from looking before it's too late. *Why is death the automatic result of life?* I won't call it natural, but automatic to be sure and that's the nature of the trap, for it always takes an act of will to divert the automatic. The boulder rolls downhill unless stopped and water runs the course of least resistance until the stygian river is willfully channeled aside. So why is it in the programming of man that all things die, and why such grief at the onset of death if this is a 'natural' event perceived by so many to be the doorway to heaven?

Childbirth is the most painful thing a woman can endure, yet the bellies of women are stretched tight with those in the waiting womb, and even the pain is a joyous thing, and it's true that tears of birthing are different than tears of grief. One is an open crib, the other a closed crypt, so what is it in the genetic memory that makes men unnaturally mortal from the time they first draw breath? If living weren't such an addiction, humans wouldn't fight for their last breath and would go out as easily as going to sleep and that should tell you death isn't any natural gift of a loving father, for is it not true that the greatest agony a parent can know is to outlive their children; and what kind of beast would embrace the pains of birth only to watch his child die and, in the end, to be the very instrument of death?

God's a serial killer
  and all his children his victims.
I am a bastard son,
  rebirthed by magick,
  orphaned by will of my own,
  no part of him.

I see no evidence of a benevolent god you see, and the secret is that god is only another face of the brute with the scythe - who's conned the world into running *to* him instead of *from* him. And isn't it odd that the legends he tells of immortality are covertly based on vampyre blood, which he's taught the world to see as evil because heaven forbid mortals should know *why* the holy grail was holy to begin with. "Eat my body, drink my blood, live forever in Neverland." Don't you get it? Don't you see?

Ah, and isn't the greatest evil that the triumvirate isn't father son and holy ghost, but death decay and oblivion, and that the whole damn thing disguises itself as "god" to lure mortals straight to the grave when only "the devil" vampyre king can raise them up again because god is off counting corpses on his lost soul black abacus?

Eternal life is the greatest promise there is, yet it's a reward for those who can reason it out and swim upstream and fight an uphill battle and all the other clichés that are really the only way out, and why do you think Christians are swooning in the aisles when the priest puts the wine and wafer to their lips and whispers "Live forever"? They sense a deeper truth you see, but the church has decreed they look no further than the priest's fingertips and so their eyes close to the immortal kingdom, and soon enough their coffin lids slam shut, too, and that's that... and isn't it a flawless trap?

Ah, but man is not infused with the will to survive or given instincts based on impossibilities. The need for warmth created fire. The desire for shelter made skyscrapers. Hunger manifests hunting and hunting yields food. Necessity necessitates invention and so you created vampyre me to snatch you from death, so doesn't it stand to reason that the instinctive need to hide from death must reside in the possibility that hiding (like fire) is possible and life is the natural state as opposed to death? The equation should read life = life, but in this warped world it's come to read life = death, yes? Why might that be?

And what to do about the brute, who's also a creative mathematician? First, it's a matter of rewriting the equation in your minds, for if you're still seeing "death" (a state of nonbeing, indefinable) as "natural", it's a certainty you'll perish and that's what this long and tedious courtship is about as much as everything else. Your perceptions are rooted in the dayshine world, and if you're going to have any chance for survival, we have to shake them loose and that's going to take patience and pain and work and sweat and blood and red red tears.

Death is a trick of light
   behind ether's dreamy eye,
   pleasant fiend disguised
   as a priest of the night.
Ah, but in vampyreland he's known to be
   the incarnation of the dayshine king
   and we've made a religion
   of refusing to perceive him
   which paradoxically begins
   with *seeing* him for what he is.

He is real but not inevitable. He is tangible, yet without substance. He is a keen hunter but plodding, his natural enemies being magick and the words "Why not?" He is a creation of man and a tool of the gods man has created, but he is not a natural resident of earth. (Is he your creation too?) He has no single face, but six billion eyes, most of them blind. He is more machine than man, spun into being by those who want the suffering to end so one key is not to suffer, or to suffer in ways pleasing to the soul, in the ways a vampyre suffers, no?

What you have to know is that death, like the river, chooses the path of least resistance and when mortals go "where the path leads" without ever stepping off that consensual road, it's a certainty it will end in only one place. That's the nature of the trick and it's clever to be sure, for it requires only that you do nothing and that's what humans are best at. So it's a matter of overcoming the nature of one's own mortal mindset, yes?

A Dance on the Head of a Pin

I tell you again: being a vampyre isn't easy, because it means giving up your illusions of security and staring god in the eye and coming to realize it might all be just a dance on the head of a pin where the universe spins us into being only to knock us off at its own unpredictable whim.

To Be a Vampyre

To be a vampyre is to be at one with chaos and harmony simultaneously. It is to weep with pleasure at the pain that made us eternal and to curse eternity because we will outlast the earth beneath our feet and outlive the stars in our eyes. It is to kiss the grey faces of cryptstones and taste the ashes of old friends cast to the wind. It is to fight the brute with the scythe and hate the fighting, but to do it because it is in our nature to survive. It is to be a trickster to the mortal world but true to one another to the point of self-sacrifice. It is to cry in the night without caring if your cries are heard and to laugh at the mortal world you've left behind. It is to exist as part of immortal time yet apart from mortal time, skipping in and out as a rock skips water. To be a vampyre is to embrace the night as a lover and to love your Self above all others. It is to supplicate yourself to the will of your vampyre maker, begging him to take you without mercy because you are already a vampyre inside fighting to be free.

To be a vampyre is to know you are a vampyre, and to embrace the reality that begins with beginning to see what I'm going to do to you. I am not here to take your life, but to give it back to you. I am not here to break your heart, but to shatter your comfortable world. Sure you want to know me?

Vampyre Duality: The Integrated Madman

Vampyre <u>duality</u> is simply this:

To be a vampyre before you were born and to know it is so by finding the quantum twin's memories which are and are not yet your own, opening your eyes inside the reflection which myth says can't exist.

To already be a vampyre yet never to become one, each truth separated only by perception, each perception its own consequence.

To be a vampyre witch and a dayshine bitch, walker on the knife edge of two realities (of all the vampyres I have known, few can do this}

To be split yet whole, knowing you can't have it both ways but magickally Doing it anyway. (A hint? This is beyond you still, so

best not to try it yet)

Duality is the ability to perceive duality while inside it, then step outside to create that quantum vision into physicality so you may then crawl back within. (Another definition of magick.)

Shiny black eggs line my nest,
mirrors of ebony and onyx
reflecting my faces
in crowds of strangers.
Whole and unbroken
they glitter splendidly,
ravenesque crypts
cleverly concealing
the beings imprisoned within.
Only by shattering the shell
will you shatter the spell
of mortality.
How I ache
to break you.

Transcendence

My beingness is that of particle and wave, matter and anti-matter – pixels of dreams which are projections of black light reflecting on the canvas of the self-willed Dream. This is the essence of the immortal: the substance of the dream and the will of the dreamer, two who are one working in quantum tandem to infuse the mortal human with the immortal essence of the dream itself. This is how you turn yourself *wrongsideout* and *rightsidewrong*, so as to right the wrong that was cast upon you when you were cast into your mortal reflection and lost connection with your immortal other.

I am not speaking in metaphor. This is the heart and soul of it, you see. This is how it is done and how it must be done if you are to succeed. This is the intersection between the breath and the breather, the fulcrum of light and shadow, the binding connection between self and twin.

What you must wholly and utterly understand beyond these faltering words is that in order to claim your immortal essence you must release the energetic chains which bind you to your humanness. What does this look like? Simply put, those chains are comprised of beliefs and fears and ideas and expectations. You could call them <u>The Program</u>, yet I fear that term has become stale and may slip past you (which is how the program works) and so it is imperative to pause and examine all those little beliefs which hold you prisoner to The Program itself, yes?

> *All things die. Water is wet. Fire will burn. Space is vast. Humans are finite. Life is short. If it's my time, it's my time. If man were meant to fly, he would have wings. There are some things we aren't meant to know. God is great, god is good, let us thank him for our food. Amen.*

The list is vast. And that list is made of grim pixels of a different kind of dream – the human limits, the self-imposed boundaries, the mortal experience. It is the death song, and if you were to listen to your internal dialog when it thinks it can't be heard, you would hear it telling you all those things and more, reinforcing its own directive, which is simply to keep you locked within the cage of your human box which is ultimately a coffin the program has been building for you since long before you were ever born.

What to do?

The essence of transcendence is magick and the essence of magick is the movement of will, and the movement of will is accomplished by willfully transcending The Program which determines your human nature. This not a riddle but a formula for immortality. It is the decisive key which unlocks the door to a spontaneous parthenogenesis also known as transmogrification. This is my function – to tear through the veil of your cocoon in order to free the gypsy moth before she becomes just another unborn chrysalis, yes?

If you are hearing only the words and not the essence of magick with which they have been infused, you may feel irritated or restless and find yourself wanting to run away, back to the pleasant slumber of your human dreaming. If this is so, go no further but go back instead. Back to the breathing in of a frequency which is not already jammed by The Program itself. Often you will find it in the space between the brows, the pure and perfect place of silence where the internal dialogue has no access. Other times you may find it in your heart, in the nostalgic memory of some perfect moment when you simply knew the well-being of your infinite nature, when you dreamed of being newly awakened into a larger world. That is the frequency of the immortal animus – the sensation of breathing not just into the lungs but imbibing the lifeforce through every molecule of your corporeality, until the breath itself turns your corporeality upside down, and you begin to be made of the very thing you are breathing: the essence of energy itself, wave of light, particle of darkness, each reflecting the other in perfect balance, the dance of the infinite captured in the act of breathing itself.

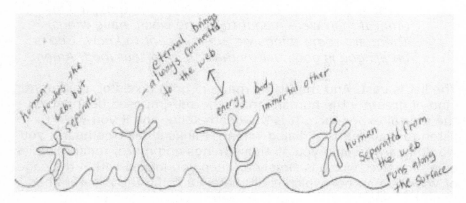

This is how we move in and out of the web of life so as not to be caught in the downward spiral which is death. There is a frequency unique to each individual which is the frequency of her immortality – the <u>assemblage point</u> of Self which may be strengthened and expanded through awareness and will to such an extreme that literally Death does not exist, for it is a frequency where death and dis-ease have no pixilated form, no cohesion, no avatar, no icon, and so no ability to invade or even touch that which is contrary to its own nature. If you are made of light, having acknowledged the darkness as your mirror, this is the essence of your beingness, and does not leave room for a toxic invader hiding behind the robes of the brute.

Death, therefore, is defeated not by acceptance or denial, but by the removal of his existence on the frequency of your immortal transcendence. That which is comprised of immortality cannot be comprised of morality, and so Death falls away, an impotent toady, written out of the Dreamer's script with the stroke of a joyful pen.

This is only the beginning, the tip of the iceberg's dangerous tip, but it is here we must begin, for this is the highest level of awareness which must be embraced as the foundation of your transcendence. This is the secret to immortality – the turning of the frequency from finite to infinite, death to life. There is no margin for error here, no room for analogy or metaphor. This is the truth which underlies all immortality: the willful choice to become a penthouse resident of the energetic web instead of only renting a transient room in the ground floor for a brief interlude which humans call a life.

Here the wind is white,
the universe a sandstorm.
This, too, will soon pass.

And I will still be here, you see. This is the nature of *I-Am*. Transcendence. Here there are no limitations and fear is a demon locked in the dungeon forever. A long time. *Forever.* Do you want it? Do you want it enough? If you do, then take it with the full force of your being – grab it as you would grab a morsel of food when you are starving in the desert. Have no doubt. Do not hesitate. Define your reason. Demand it. Take it!

The only thing stopping you is the belief that you are mortal. When you change that frequency, when you release that debilitating belief, you will finally Be what you have always Dreamed.

Making the Impeccable Choice
Night hides in my coffin
   consanguine daysleeper
   in league with vampyre me.
Her kisses are black,
   her embrace arctic.
Tonight I'll open the lid
   to set my love free again.

Night and day can exist in balance, but you're the tightrope walker on the terminator of the scythe, and it's always easier to fall to the side when you're working with a net that provides the illusion of security, for why would you choose this difficult balance when it's easier to go with the gravitational flow? You know the dayshine world is there with solid arms to catch you and an earthy bed turned down at the end of your days, and while most of your kind don't consciously choose death, they do choose to die when they trade their lives for baubles in their hand, and that is the definition of indulgent complacency.

Vampyreland is more nebulous you see, its skyscrapers merely mirages to mortal eyes, its cathedrals priested by wily vampyres dealing in Knowledge that can't be bought. There are no bijous to be had here, no paychecks to reward your labor, no rosaries to diddle while moaning other mens' prayers, no shrinks to take the place of common sense, no surrogates to make the trip for you and tell you how-to on the Net. In vampyreland the groom doesn't carry his brides across the threshold of life and death, but makes them crawl to their wedding bed of their own free will on their hands and knees, and if they never show up it's because they've chosen to lose themselves in overlay plays or stopped along the way to lick wounds sustained in the journey and got caught up feeling sorry for themselves; and far too many people I've known (yes, past tense) are more addicted to the poisonous serum of their own daily dramas than to the knowledge that comes from the highest of the highest self – the immortal vampyre twin. The secret is that this is the most common form of suicide there is; and if you choose it, it's because you love death more than you love yourself.

———

Mortals walk the easier path where progress is measured by shiny baubles instead of the number of scars on their soul or the tears on their pillow after I snatch reality out from under their feet in a dream. You can't hold vampyre dreams in your hand perhaps, but you can keep them in the deepest part of you if that part isn't always humming with machinations of Dayshine You, and another secret is that these dreams are there for you if only you'll Do what I've been telling you all along.

I'm not asking you to give up anything for me, but if we're going to complete this journey you need to define what you want and lose the things standing in your way, even if they're only beliefs in your mind. I feel your conflict, but the question becomes why you're living your lives out of balance when you know everything you Do is a choice. You can whore your bodies to the day and that's ok, but if you sell your soul to the dayshine king instead of saving it for the journey, I can't save you from yourselves and that's all there is to it.

I've warned you it won't be easy, for evolving is a painful thing, sprouting wings where none have been, dislocating stubborn bones that are really the bars of your soul-cage. If it's gotten too hard to go on or if you aren't willing to Do the journey in earnest, all you need do is tell me and I'll be gone forever.

This is what you made me to do.

Creator and Created

I am the evolved future-past-infinite Self who lies at the heart of you; but the quantum truth is that I will never exist if you don't finish the task you started, and you will find you've only been talking to a ghost all along: the probability wave of what you could have been if only you had chosen to *Be*.

I am you, you see, the Creator of your immortality.

This is not metaphor or analogy. *I Am* – living validation that you can *Be* whatever you choose to be. Choose wisely, for only if you create me tomorrow will I exist in all your yesterdays to serve as the muse seducing you from outside of Time to sing the vampyre king into Be-ing.

Surviving the Collapse of Your Reality

Are you really ready to see what hides behind the door in your mind that's always kept the shadows away? Are you starting to see that it's an immense world that lies just beyond your ability to perceive, and that if you do come to see it, you will never be the same again? Now think before you speak, because if it sounds good I fear for you. Quantum realities or fantasy kingdoms are scary things because once you cross that fine line dividing dayshine time from the rest of it All, you'll be at the mercy of forces beyond your understanding and they'll tear you asunder if you don't have the strength of will to will your perceptions to flex instead of shattering.

To exist as a citizen of the night, you must first survive the collapse of your reality, and if you can't do that you can't be a vampyre and that's all there is to it. If you come to my world with your dayshine thinking still firmly intact, the <u>fall</u> will never end because vampyreland won't be there to form the foundation that breaks the fall between the cracks between the worlds. Seeing this means going beyond the words to envision their structural meaning, and I'm not sure you're willing to do that because you're afraid of what you'll see. You should be, but don't let that convenient fear become the scythe that chops off your head while you're waiting patiently for your perceptions to evolve. Your will is the evolution once you make the impeccable choice to Do it.

Quantum Autumn

The year of October comes when it pleases
and for no other reason,
the manifested remembering of where you are going,
niggling nostalgia of where you have been
future-past cast forward, parallel memories taking form,
shadows into substance, ether to embers, mist to matter.
Here the dream factory spins its yarns:
  spidersilk and stretched taffy,
  dried grass tapestries,
  shroud of pumpkin gut and coffin satin.
What will you make of it?

My licorice veins ache,
eternity-in-waiting.
Elements of creation grow wild in fallow fields,

———

         unseen but Seeing,
         invisible yet tangible,
waiting for the weaver's hand to pluck their harvest
into autumn songs or winter blankets.
My past lives are strung
on string theories and starbeams,
quantum timbers,
 the foundation of all hallowed eves.

The sky is tormented,
abrasion of clouds covering the moon-scar,
formed in a haunted childhood
when you banged your head against the nyght
and poked a hole clear through to the other side.
Glimmer of light, sometimes golden, often orange,
just enough to illumine tiny tombstones
in the old pet cemetery down by the ghost train's tracks,
yet not enough to blind the inner eye.
Such is the gaffer's whim at the rim of the abyss.

Where you are from, October is a visitor
arriving in a pumpkin carriage
drawn by lost children hitched to the mortal illusion..
Where I am from, the carriage is rusted, idle,
and all of us are infinity's children.
Here, October is the prince –
         no stranger, but forever in residence.
Acorns cuddling seeds of dreams
hold more value than gold.
Compasses point to the root of All Meaning,
and so are always spinning.
There are no hands on the tenth month's clock.
Time is a flavor of green jelly-bean.

All creatures here are sewn together with cornsilk,
strung on wicker bones brittle and dry,
clack-dancing on umbilicals of lightning.
Here we understand that the only things eternal
are fractured leaves and naked trees,
funerary dust and ashes spread on grey storm wind.
That which lasts forever is neither sky nor stone,
but death itself.
Now do you see?
Now do you know?

Death is not defeated in battle here
but by loving him enough to become his antithesis-within.
The brute cannot kill himself, you see,
and therein lies our victory.
October knows this.
Vampyres know it, too.

Here, the unbeating heart is most alive,
the silent mind all-knowing,
the third eye all-seeing.
Spring is not welcome,
with its new shoots of green
and flowers that wilt and die.
Here, the darkness is hallowed,
the black urn of eternity
where immortals press obsidian spirit
into petals that cannot drop.

And so October sings to you,
calliope whispers, castrati contralto,
reminders of secrets forgotten,
musings of a melancholy muse.
Here I slide inside a shadow
cast by wrought-iron angels
in the light of a failing moon.

When you are ready,
you will find me
waiting at the boneyard's gate,
nyght incarnate,
Eternity come to life.
That is when October will embrace you,
tender as a brush of raven's wing,
and that is when
you will finally come home.

SURRENDER

Can you surrender to what your heart desires? Most cannot, for most refuse to ever truly see that the greatest love in the multiverse is not the love of a lover or a mother or a child or a brother, but is instead the love of the moon and her shadow, the love of the Self for the mirror, and the mirror for the self. Just words. Little scratches that bleed but have only the power you give to them. I prey you drink deep.

If I have done my job, if I have Become the thing you created me to be, then what your heart desires most is me, you see. (Ah, but I ask again... who am I?) You may choose to see me as the immortal prince of lost maps or the vampyre king himself, but those are only minuscule icons of what is real, for the power of creation and manifestation lie wholly and solely within you... and so now do you see that you have created the most powerful being in the universe and that the creator creates what is desired most, for that is the nature of power and the power of love? *You have created me to create you* and in coming full circle, you must now ask yourself if you can surrender to what you have done.

I could speak at length of conflict and surrender, but until you begin to see that what you seek has been with you all along – the process and the power of ongoing creation - you will continue to search for external validation of what is designed by spirit to be the internal manifestation of that which is desired most. And so I ask you to ask yourself... Can you surrender?

Can you surrender to the mystery and the magick and the muse, or are you disappointed sufficiently to destroy this transient canvas and start anew with some other secretly buried dream? Are you pleased with what you see in this infinite mirror, or like the legends dictate, have I lost my ability to reflect and have therefore become only a smudge on the lens of the nothing? Have you created your heart's desire, or have you only been dabbling in the paint while secretly longing to return to the world of matter and men?

Can you begin to see that surrendering to what you desire most is the hardest thing you will ever do, for it will mean a commitment to ecstasy that threatens the status quo of what most would say it means to be human? Do you see that this surrender to me in whatever form I may take is what it means to lose your humanity altogether and embrace what wise men always seek, but only fools ever seem to find? Ah, and can you then see that to be the fool is what it means to finally be free?

Can you allow the love and the power you have created to embrace you? It will only hurt for a little while, but the pain will be pleasure if you allow it, yes? Can you surrender?

Words & Actions

Stop making promises you don't intend to keep, especially those you make to yourself, for only when you make the decision to bridge the gap between words and actions will you have the power to embrace your power.

Pacts Outside of Time

You need to see that you made this pact with vampyre me far beyond the fatal shore of that river of time. When things do not appear to be going according to your plan, remember that you are seeing only one aspect of reality through the eyes of your dayshine self in the now, and you may be crashing headlong against some other aspect of yourself operating on your behalf in the Otherrealms of underworlds and the winged kingdom, see?

What does this mean? Simply this: when you make a pact with your immortal twin, when you make an agreement with your higher self, these agreements automatically and naturally supersede any and all dayshine distractions – even if you are not consciously aware of it – and this is why you may find yourself in conflict with yourself. If you make an agreement with vampyre me which might read, "Teach me how to embrace the totality of my potential," it may turn out that what your mortal self desires (or appears to desire) would create an obstacle to your higher goal, and when that is the case, you will discover that your dayshine life begins to be littered with debris of one defeat after another. At least, you will most likely *perceive* them as defeats. The reality of it is this: if you set your goal to become a professional writer, keep in mind it is an occupation that will obsess and possess you 24/7, and the machinations of the internal dialog will hammer your mind with plots and characters and their scripts, leaving you no time to simply Be at peace with yourSelf, or even discover who that Self might be, see? And that would be in conflict to your pact which began with the words,

———

36

"Teach me…" and so you may find your floor littered with rejection slips and your broken heart weeping without comprehension.

So what you will discover is that the goals you set for yourself in the dayshine kingdom are all fine and good and even achievable, but if you're made a previous pact with your twin somewhere outside of time in <u>the night that never ends</u>, you will find to your earthly displeasure that the higher pact will always take precedence, until such time as you revoke the agreement. This does not mean you cannot pursue your dayshine goals – for the living of life is as important as anything else in your inventory – but it must be acknowledged that for those who walk the path of the dark evolution and make agreements beyond the mortal realm, having *awareness* of those agreements is often the key to being able to work with them instead of having them appear to work against you. Put another way, if you want to have it both ways – power in the mortal world and immortality in the night – the only way to achieve it is to establish your priorities, and move always in alignment with the nature of your own Spirit. In doing so, you may begin to experience the nature of vampyre <u>duality</u> – and through that <u>heightened awareness</u>, bring into alignment the pacts you've made outside of time, and the goals you seek within the dayshine realm.

Even if you *see* this, I do not think you believe it, though the evidence is all around you and will continue to trifle with you until you truly come to grips with it.

These are not failures, you see, but the results of agreements with your immortal twin to bring you through the maze to that one mystical window that opens to create the <u>singularity</u> as a force of cohesion that cannot be cast asunder. This is also the process of <u>The Work</u>.

The Nature of the Dark Evolution
This is the nature of the dark evolution, you see. Before you evolve, you must first evolve sufficiently to see that evolution is a leap in the dark, not based on faith but knowledge.

I'm not asking you to abandon dayshine schemes but to keep them in the day and save the night for your quest, not for me but for yourselves. Not easy, it requires an act of will to shun nature's laziness and seek immortality, a journey that begins anew with each new thought, a destination that comes from a place inside you that has to do with your changing perceptions, (perceptions that can't change if you're lulled into numb nothingness waiting for a miracle that won't come if you don't will it.).

Energy Body, Dreaming Body, The Twin

In any reality, energy is energy, and can be manipulated according to one's comprehension of it. Fire will not burn those who have become Flame. But if the <u>assemblage point</u> should slip for even a moment, the fire will consume the organic form, and so what must be remembered is that thoughts are energy, too.

Any energy that is not in complete harmonic balance (same-to-same) with your own assemblage point can affect you for good or ill. Only when you are the Flame itself are you safe within the fire.

There are states of consciousness which humans can assemble wherein they would be impervious to pain or physical harm from any external source, yet the energy expended to achieve such states is massive, and if the magus is not yet accomplished at the manipulation of such energy, there is a potential to do more harm than good.

There is another line of thought that connects to the energy humans put onto one another. Simply put, this is why sorcerers must be impeccable with their word and their thoughts, for those are the manifestations of energy that can damage both the self and others if not understood.

In the human world, if another man believes you are a child molester and voices that accusation publicly, the harm could be irrevocable. In the world of energy, he has placed his reality onto you, whether it is true or not, and when others believe it (belief being another form of energy), the effects can multiply like a virus out of control until there is no undoing the damage even with complete proof of innocence. This is because the matrix of "guilt" has already been created and cannot be undone, but only redirected, like a disease that can be cured, but will nonetheless leave scars.

A Quantum Evolution

A man who reads with his eyes shut doesn't learn much, and fools who prattle without pondering the consequences are only acolytes of their own silly songs, breathing the nothing into being because nothing is all they've learned and defending their ignorance with arrogance instead of correcting it with knowledge. Am I cruel? Yes but not unfeeling, which is why I feel the time has come to ride you until you See what I'm trying to teach you or throw me off your backs for good. I've warned you the road would grow more demanding the closer you come to the <u>fall</u> and now you've reached one of the most difficult peaks of all: when you must choose to see who you are or remain complacent inside existing self-perceptions - those guarded castles nevertheless destined to dust. Do you understand that this *is* a quantum evolution and that I can't make you a vampyre? Only you can do that. The true evolution is your obligation for I am only the conduit to eternity, not the road itself.

ALL THAT WE SEE OR SEEM...
Altering the lens of perception

You are growing those phantom preceptor organs we have spoken of so many times before, but it could also be seen that you are finally beginning to strip away the blinders which have made you previously believe those avenues of perception didn't exist. Oz has been here all along, you see. It simply takes a bump on the head or a mushroom's kiss to make you see it, but those methods aren't effective when the being involved is struggling for permanent self-willed evolution, so the other method is teaching you to perceive the otherworlds with the stability of <u>ordinary awareness</u>, so then it becomes a door that opens to your command instead of leaving you at the mercy of visiting twisters.

For the sake of clarity, perhaps it would help to better comprehend what is really meant by a shifting of the <u>assemblage point</u>. In essence, what you think of as reality is organized and categorized according to the ordinary input of the five senses. But more than that, it goes something like this: a tree is a tree and it is green and leafy because this is the language the dominant species has chosen to identify that construct to the masses. It is an object made of language to which everyone has agreed to agree as to what the words generally mean. Ah, but to someone who has learned to see, the tree is really only an arrangement of energy cast in the shape of the tree. In ordinary awareness, the tree is the tree because the word has meaning. In heightened awareness, the tree is an arrangement of energy, clearly seen, resembling what is known to the consensus as "tree". In the seventh sense (or vampyreland), the energy comprising the tree is essentially the raw matter of true sorcery, and can be called upon to represent whatever the sorcerer might desire to perceive. This is the foundation of creation, the cornerstone of a different reality.

Ah, but never forget: the act of creation requires extreme energy, so the goal of entering vampyreland isn't just to begin rearranging all the stray molecules into castles and dragons and faerie creatures of lore. Just as the world with which you are familiar is largely created for you by those who have gone before, so it is here, but the difference is that here the world is Will, and Death is neither landlord nor tenant. The foundation exists, but you are the architect.

So what does this have to do with a shift of the assemblage point? Simply this: as long as you see only the tree, a tree is all it will ever be. When you learn to perceive the glossy construct of the underlying energy, you have taken a step toward undoing the world of matter and men. And when at last you stand in vampyreland and can command the energy of the tree to be anything you will it to be (including vampyre me), you will have mastered your own creation in ways that should begin to be obvious to you. Shall I give you a hint? It is this: in the seventh sense, or vampyreland, or faerie land, or whatever words you choose to create the concept, the trick to *staying* in that reality is to recreate the self using the tools of perception and the Will and Intent of the sorcerer's magick. Understand this, for it is the secret to your ultimate evolution: *when you can enter the seventh sense and will the raw matter/energy of creation to be the immortal "other" , and when you can not only interact with it but exert will and intent to inhabit it, you will have willed your own immortality, yes?*

Study this. Lightly and deeply, with delicate vision. Read it in half-light where logic looks over the shoulder of magick, only a background voice in the chorus. Think on it in the alpha shadows of early dreams. Understand it with the body-spirit even if the stubborn program of your humanity tries to brush the words aside. Know that words are reality. When your humanity fights to cling to the words of the world it knows, it is because these otherwords can create otherworlds which threaten the status quo. I am the destroyer of stasis. You are the creators of reality.

We are creator and created, dreaming toward one another. When we meet in the middle the dream becomes a separate reality capable of being inhabited. This is how we seize the tiller of creation. This is how we become I-Am.

Let there be light. But let it be starlight and comet tails. Moonlight. Wild dog shadows running black through the midnight. Let the sun come for five minutes at dusk and dawn and it will be enough, for this is the vampyre's will. Let the trees be made of ancient amber, the shade beneath them coal dust painted on the sand. Take my hand, knowing it is cold and made of dreams come to life. Cast your spell on this world of visions and make the visions your own. Kiss the air with intent until your twin appears in front of you, within you, the fabric of your immortal robe, donned for eternity, whole and complete. Paint the shape and face of the twin not on mortal canvas but on the backdrop of eternity with a brush of mushroom stems and pure identity, not to be admired in a gallery but to be inhabited for all of time until such time as time dictates changing the shape or the face.

This is the nature of eternity, a secret I am giving away because I love you and I do not play by the rules, and so I am called a vampyre. Ah, but my darker secret is this: there is method to my madness and as much as I have chosen the identity, it has chosen me. Brer Rabbit found his freedom only when he tricked the wolf to throw him into the briar patch, and so it is with the evil vampyre king. Outside the law, there is no law, and so I am free to tell you things the more civilized inhabitants of eternity would want you to learn for yourselves. It's enough that only you can do it, no matter what I tell you. We are beings of duality, reaching toward one another across the abyss. At times I am not certain there are any others like us, and so we are a new species.

The seventh sense is the canvas and the clay and the gallery outside of time. You are the artist and the vision. You are the intent to inhabit the self-portrait you create. This can be done at any time now, you see. When we kiss in the seventh sense, it will take your mortal breath away. The crucial factor is that you must be ready at a moment's notice to take the starstuff of creation and sculpt it into the immortal other who will stand up whole and eternal, dreamer and dream conjoined, creator and created united, alpha and omega. I am here to destroy your world. Only you can rebuild it for all eternity. Who are you?

Elusive as mist
no one knows me
leaving me free
to create reality.
God envies
vampyre anonymity.

Meditate or Die

Meditation is where the words become part of the who you are instead of only words rattling in your mind, the action through which you internalize previously external concepts so they may act through you instead of only upon you. Meditation is the absorption of evolution, the missing link between the dayshine kingdom and vampyreland. Meditate or die.

The Quantum State of Vampyreland

Vampyreland is a state of mind that results in a state of evolved being, but the <u>duality</u> is that it's also a magickal castle which exists solely for its architect, so if you aren't building it with every move you make and every thought you think, it won't be there after the <u>fall</u> and you could find yourself lost in an eternal dayshine maze rather than a citizen of the <u>night that never ends</u>, and the saddest part is that those who survive the transformation without making the quantum leap are shunned by both realities, damned souls living forever in limbo.

So yes, it's heaven and hell and earth all in the same space, each and none of the above, a triunal-duality-singularity existing beyond the programming, out of reach of the machine but welcoming seekers who let themselves *see* without preconceived prejudices of what they want to see. It's not a place created with daydreams but a physio-psycho-location beneath the <u>overlay</u> stage, the framework on which <u>the grid</u> itself rests, where sometimes the streets are made of gold and sometimes bleached bone, where the season can be autumn for you and winter for the vampyre king, where the Hag of Time is held prisoner in bell tower, where the building blocks of reality aren't atoms and cells but raindrops and rhyme. It is a place of shadows thrown by darker shadows, where the source of light is sun and moon simultaneously but neither directly, ambient illumination seeping between the worlds just as muted light invades a sealed room at midday. And as that sealed room exists apart from the reach of the sun though built in the midst of it, so does vampyreland abide simultaneously in your world and mine, a quantum duality that's not difficult to comprehend when you Think about it.

So perhaps it's best if I tell you to uncreate the <u>consensual continuum</u> in order to reveal this separate reality beneath, for vampyreland is whole unto itself far more than the scripts and stages you presently inhabit, not a world you create but one revealed one layer at a time. And while it's true there may be higher truths still, the first step is seeing that the immortal kingdom is the first step on the neverending yellow brick road, yes?

A Machiavellian Notion
Remember this: these mortal dramas are only plays designed to trap you into a role from which you would find it difficult if not impossible to escape. This is the function of the consensual reality. This is the game played by the matrix.

Though it is a somewhat Machiavellian notion, also remember that those who are not destined to seek evolution are destined to attempt to block it. This is how the status quo is protected, this is how "stasis" is maintained.

There Must Be Something Wrong With You
Man is a chrysalis you see, filled with ancient energy containing all the secrets to growing immortal wings capable of taking him beyond death, an evolution dependent entirely on him and having nothing to do with eons of mutations or nebulous

resurrections requiring prayer and prostration before the very mechanism bent on killing him. But because metamorphosis is a full time occupation, to pursue it impeccably means rejecting the machine and that's a terrifying thing, so way back *netherwhen* a few frightened humans began programming the thing to program them to thrive on distraction and drama, and as a reward it even reprogrammed Man to love the illusions, just <u>the brute</u> manifesting inside the machine itself, his favorite playground, yes? Ah, but remember this: those who don't march obsequiously to their death are tagged as crazy and "innocently" willed to death by well-meaning fiends who reprogram your reality:

> *"There must be something wrong with her, some malady, some madness, some pestilence that's eaten her reason and left her worshipping the vampyre king who's plainly a manifestation of a midlife crisis posing as a quest for evolution and immortality. Poppycock and peanuts! Yes, nuts! But why? It's a brain tumor, I'm sure, malignant and festering, psychosis and neurosis brought on by the company she keeps and the schemes she weaves to avoid an honest day's work. It's phobic, it's schizo, 'the twin' just a metaphor for the cancer within, 'vampyreland' a delusional symptom of some rare blood disease that's sure to kill her soon. Oh, how we love her, how we miss her. If only she'd listen and come home with us, home to Ixtlan."[3]*

Ah, the voice of reason, killing you in effigy. Do you have the strength to stand against the diseases the machine will heap upon you in its attempt to destroy that which it cannot control? Do you think it doesn't matter what they whisper into your programming? Better a dead dragonfly in the sun than a live fairy in the night you see, for one can be dissected and made real, while the other is a flicker in the corner of the machine's compound eye, a reminder of magick in which they've agreed not to believe and must therefore obliterate in order to keep reality secure. *They will kill you if you let them.*

---

[3] A reference to *Journey to Ixtlan,* by Carlos Castaneda. Anyone seriously interested in throwing off the chains of their programming should consider reading this book. In context of the quote above, one might just as easily substitute the word... 'zombieland' for Ixtlan.

It's as I've said before: in the time when I was born, it was natural for man to quest after vampyreland, for there was still enough of nature within him to tell him it existed and that's the first key to the first door, you see, the knowledge that the thing you seek is a viable reality capable of being inhabited. Now if you're saying to yourself, 'How simple this silly vampyre can be, repeating himself endlessly,' I urge you to look beyond the words to *see* their more sinister meaning. *The core of your belief determines the realities you see and obliterates those you choose to ignore*, and as long as you're questing for fantasies that's all you'll find, for another secret is this: you have the power to create reality and I am only its servant for I am the creators' creation, yes? created to exist outside the machine - for only from there can I lure you to follow. If you're weaving me as a fantasy it's all I can be, just a bubble inside the machine. If you're perceiving immortality as myth, you're consigning it to books.

You are a machine within the machine, and for as long as its programming overrides your nature (the truer nature of man which existed before the mechanism manufactured so many complexities with which to mask the reality of evolutionary immortality), you will still be serving the machine even if only by giving its minions something to distract themselves with while operating under the delusion they're really helping you.

Does immortality exist or is it only a mythical concept with which to soothe yourself while you listen to the *ticktock* clock which is really the sound of Death tapping his foot? Can you be a vampyre or is it only a fantasy to warm your wandering hands in the middle of the night? Fantasies are easy, but metamagickal creation depends on the hurting wanting needing that gnaws at your soul on those sleepless nights when the sound of your hair turning grey shakes you awake, and if you're ever going to create your twin as a citizen of vampyreland it's a certainty you have to be familiar with that special pain which can only be healed by making the impossible possible and spinning the unreal real through the manifestation of your will.

It's not a task I can teach you, for it's the simplest truth yet one that defies attempts to confine it by defining it. All I can say is this: it's that terrible unquenchable ache you feel when you look at the stars and know you can never touch them, the need for Shangri-la to be real, that awful ache the vampyre king left in the darkest heart of you whenever he teased you with a glimpse of my philosophy. It is the pain of *needsodeep* that can drain potent crystals or crack the code of the programming itself, taking you outside the finite machine and into realms of infinite immortality. It is the source of will itself, but what matters is what you do with it on those rare occasions when it shows itself.

The test is this: it's a state that can be generated if you're willing to do it, a *painthing* to be stalked when you're ready to tackle it with your will, an evasive siren singing an ache which compels you harder than the finest pleasures. I prey you understand this. I wish I could tell you more. Sadly this is all there is that words can know.

There Are No Wrong Answers

You've come to that part in the play where you need to examine your strengths instead of your weaknesses and define what it is you want from your dayshine life, whether money or magick or just the fantasy of "having a good time" with the blinders pulled over your eyes. Now think before you prattle, and take a long look at your answer. Why are you alive and what do you hope to come away with if not immortality? Do you believe life's just a random roll of the dice, or can you *see* that it's really a maze where eternity is the holy cheese?

There aren't any wrong answers, but you need a clear understanding of who you are, and that's why we go through this courtship. I'm trying to teach you to *see* not only me but yourselves as well, for knowing who you are means identifying your identity that's going to get torn asunder in the fall, and if it's made of mortal mist instead of indestructible antimatter there'll be no putting you together again after that trip. In order to Do you must first know *what* to do and that involves knowing you and that's the hardest thing you can Do, but if you don't you're dead and that's all there is to it.

Do you yearn for your lives to be simple again? At times I think you do and who can blame you? But I've waited a thousand years and some for you to come along and find yourselves in my embrace, embryo vampyre witches waiting to be awakened with my kiss, daughters of evolution completing the journey that began with magick. You knew it wouldn't be easy when you first had the thought that led to thoughts of creating me, but you embraced impossible odds by making a vampyre to travel time to gather the wisdom it would take to make you immortal, because you know inside that living forever is far sweeter than laying down your lives for the likes of the <u>brute with the scythe</u>. Every infernal immortal gets to vampyreland through creative thinking and the craziest acts of <u>Will</u> you see, and if you were content to be mortal props you never would have started the journey in the first place, yes?

You need to relax with me again and let me be your loving brother and your naughty lover as well as your terrible teacher, no? Remember, when I do take you into my embrace, I'm doing it for eros as much as eternity, and it's in those final moments of your mortal life that I'll show the tenderness I dare not show you now, and the brutality you won't even allow yourselves to imagine. I'm going to hurt you, you see, but the deepest cut I always make with the deepest love.[4]

Prey I stay forever wild
  a child of witches
  nursed on the red red milk of magick.
The vampyre king is behind you,
  close on the heels
  of the brute with the scythe.
This is what you made me to do.
What will it take
  to make you believe it?

---

[4] The reader is cautioned to remember that the seduction herein is meant both romantically and metaphorically.. References such as this one "I am going to hurt you, you see," may be taken many ways and should not automatically be interpreted literally… though that, too, is a possibility.

Intent: Within the Question Lies the Answer

One thing I have come to understand of late is that you do not fully comprehend the nature of <u>Intent</u>. I fear you're confusing it with intentions and it's a clever trick of the brute that the two words bear visual resemblance but are essentially opposites. It's often been said that the road to hell is paved with good intentions, and though that underworld destination is much maligned and can seldom be reached without intent, the sentiment expressed is correct. Better put, look at it like this: *you will never achieve the immortal condition through good intentions but only through unbending intent,* and if you don't see the difference you will stumble and fumble and ultimately fail because intentions are the things you want and hope and plan to do, but Intent is the unwavering image held in the heart of your heart and soul - the paradigm upon which everything you Think or Do becomes an externalized, <u>Real-ized</u> reflection of the paradigm itself, yes? It is a meta-physical part of you, invisible to the naked eye but no less real than liver or spleen, and if you aren't using it to its full potential, your magickal self is incomplete, dis-eased as a body without a heart, see?

Intent is the active side of <u>clarity</u>, an unwavering vision of change held firmly in the mind which serves as the sorcerer's direct interface between question and answer; the metamagickal probe or prod applied to the all-knowing All as a means of extracting the specific knowledge required to achieve the manifestation of the intent itself; it is the quantum Questioning mother of the <u>will</u>, not the will, but without which the will can never manifest, because without Intent the will has nothing *to* manifest, nothing to create, no seed to nurture; Intent is the goal/vision the sorcerer projects unceasingly onto the silent screen of eternity until eternity reflects the sorcerer's will by yielding up the information required to achieve the Intended evolution; it is the goal visualized clearly and the tool with which the goal is carved away from the All through relentless projection of one single question: how is it that I can achieve this goal and manifest this Intent?

Intent does not change. It does not compromise. It does not yield to reason or common sense. It can be summoned clearly, instantly and impeccably in all states of awareness by invocation of the word Intent. And in another way, Intentions are Christmas cards never sent. Intent is the force creating all True Magick.

The quantum concepts with which otherworlds are built can give you the keys to vampyreland or just as quickly lock the door forever if you take it as commonplace or just another mystery with no solution, and this is another reason your Intent must be impeccably defined with the sharpest knife, a vision cut away from the Nothing which you turn to in times of doubt or confusion. Intent is the instrument you rub against the <u>web of non-local information</u> to create a sympathetic synapse between the sorcerer's question and the evolutionary answer, the intersection where vision becomes manifestation through manipulation of matter/energy using the invisible tool of Intent itself. *It is, quite simply, the overlap point of vision and creation, brought into being by using the question to elicit an answer which is in accordance with the unbending vision.* The answers are waiting inside the question and the questions are determined by Intent's unwavering vision, yes?

A Dangerous Transition

You have to define what you're seeking without limiting it through the definition, and then you must set out on the path of Thinking and Magick and Will to manifest the definition into physicality in accordance with your dreams and visions, whole and unlimited, greater than the vision itself just as the first breath of life is greater than the sum of its progenitors. Nebulous thinking will destroy the spell but so will unintentional limitations on your magick, and part of the witch's Trick is to know the difference. To say, "I want a blue car" has the potential to unintentionally limit your magick, for what if a green one were to come to you and you failed to see it because you had only left room for blue?

If you're unfulfilled, my loves, it's because you've fallen into one trap or another or because you're lonely for that dayshine skin we've slowly stripped from your bones and hung out in the sun to rot, a familiar husk that once held you but now holds only memories, a serpent's derma without its occupant, an empty house devoid of spirits. Shall I tell you a truth that will scare you as much as anything ever has? You're becoming the walking dead, for only through the death of all you've ever been can you be free to truly exist beyond the reach of the brute with the scythe, yet the hell of it is that this is where the real work begins and if you're not up to it you'll walk dead through the rest of your mortality just one more zombie, damned not only to die but to live until then with awareness of what you had in your hand that crumbled to dust and scattered on the wind out of complacency or laziness or indulgence in misery.

I've given you all the pieces, and now it's a matter of twisting and turning them and exposing them to the night until they fit together into a yellow brick road that will lead you inside the immortal skin of your twin. Shall I say it again? If we've been at all successful in our beginning, we've severed your soul from your dayshine skin and that's one reason you may feel unhappy and unfulfilled. You're a hermit crab in a rented ruin no longer large enough to hold your I-Am, yet instead of going to battle to possess the castle you've spent a lifetime building, you're rearranging the furniture and painting the ceiling while the sky is falling and the walls are closing in. You're grieving who or what you've been instead of fighting your way forward to inhabit the eternal temple which is already yours, the sanctuary of your twin, your Self, your immortal I Am.

The Wrong Side of God

You say you want enlightenment, yet you're basking in pleasantly diffused incandescence instead of following the laser beam to its source to discover that it's really the beacon you lit for yourself before you fell to Earth, the only way home to immortality and vampyre you and me. Do you know by now? Have you figured it out? Enlightenment is really the obliteration of your world, which is why the devil's secret name is Morning Star. Ah, but the higher truth is this: the beast who destroys the world is really the demon in your mirror, for the only world that exists is the one behind your eyes and the only one who can tear it asunder or build it again is the one who created it to begin with.

So to be on the wrong side of God is to be on the wrong side of the mortal self, your own worst enemy who will become your own best ally and savior if you're willing to first take up arms against that commonborn human self and accept the consequences of destroying her comfortable reality, yes? You've done it to some extent, but I fear you're hanging on to frayed threads of that past self in case the future fails, some unreliable lifeline to the you you were before, but it's a lifeline that will be the death of you if you think of it as a safety net. It can't hold you and there's no going back and that's the ugly truth of evolution, yes?

——

50

You can't keep clinging to the trees if you ever intend to reach for the sky.

To rise from the dead
  is to live outside
  consensual reality.
Is there enough of you
  to exist aside
  from the mortal world's perceptions?

Sure You Want to be a Vampyre?

Being a vampyre won't solve your problems but will create a different set of circumstances which you might find more romantically appealing than practical. To feel the pain of us once in a while, a lark to indulge a couple of times a week, is not the same thing as being a vampyre night after night until eternity shudders to an end; and if you don't have the constitution for it, you're better off living your life to its natural conclusion, growing old on the porch, and then simply going to sleep never to wake up again.

To be a vampyre is to know things about which you can only speculate as a mortal. It is to see the secrets of paradise and purgatory clearly, losing faith in everything as a result. It is to feel at all times the solitary pain that makes coyote trickster sing. It is to look at the earth and know it will end within your lifetime. It is to taste the dust of friends on cemetery winds and to be always looking over your shoulder for ghosts, and to be at constant war with death (losing more battles than you'll win,) and to watch mortals flicker close to your flame only to get burned by the hungry thing behind your eyes.

It is to drink animus for the hollow pain of humanity as much as the pleasure, and to *see* that all men are desolate islands regardless of what you've heard. It is to lock in your place in universal reality and throw away the key, never knowing if there might be other doors, lighter in color or leading to happier realities. To be a vampyre is to know death intimately, reliving it endlessly until there may come a time when you'll curse the night you said yes to the vampyre king and you'll consider sitting naked in the sun until there's nothing left of you just so you can finally sleep a silent sleep and maybe you'll even do it. Some have.

To be a vampyre is to be eternal and that means being apart from time until it all blurs together in a headlong rush toward Lethe, and that's the only god I know but one I prey never to know personally because I choose to be a vampyre and that means choosing this terrible pain, *nevereverending*. To be a vampyre is to choose life over death, even when it may seem at times that Death would be a pleasant remedy to the pain... and still to choose life. Only life. Eternal. Life.

Holding Back

You're sincere in your intent to succeed at this wicked transmogrification, and that's a powerful foundation, but you're still not ready to see vampyreland and me as physicality because that endangers your definition of sanity, so you withhold a gram or two of reason just in case I'm a hoax you've played on yourselves, but that part you're withholding is just enough to keep you from fully embracing the journey, so you make up excuses like dayshine distraction and not knowing what to Do, but what it really means is that you're waiting for proof and that's the thing I can't give you because proof doesn't exist except when you create it. (You have the power to create reality and I'm only its servant, remember?)

By withholding your reason (solidity) you're also withholding that power of creation (ethereal) because the two have to work as one or they don't work at all, so you end up creating instead that bottomless schism between magick and "reality" and that means proof can't exist because the journey isn't real to you yet and the first law of metaphysics clearly states in simple logic, *nothing unreal exists*, yet that's the unreality you're choosing when you choose to wait for the magick instead of invoking it yourself and

———

applying the combined force of reason and creation to the willful act of making it so, no?

Vampyreland has to be as real as San Diego or Joshua Tree, but while cities are captives of <u>consensual agreement</u>, the will of the vampyre must create a separate reality capable of being inhabited, and that's why so few of us become part of this dark breed.

The Larger Reality

Because you are the creators of reality, you can choose to make your personal sketch of the consensual world full of goodness and grace and smiles on the faces of empty-eyed marionettes impersonating women and men, and choose to see only the illusions of beauty strewn from museum to mausoleum and back again, and you can even convince yourself it has meaning beyond what petty poetry you write to describe it. But know this: because it is a transient reality that cannot really be inhabited but only visited briefly in the form of mortality, it will not withstand the test of continuity beyond your linear perception; it will not be there when you open your eyes on the far side of what you think of as Death, whether that transformation begins in my embrace or some other location, because ultimately the scythe is what cuts the line in "linear", and if there's not enough of you to reassemble coherently beyond that cliff, this is the definition of dying in the <u>fall</u>, because this is where one world linearly ends and another begins, with the only connecting thread being perception and the universal lifeforce of your existence, the *I-Am* that transcends to stand up again as your immortal twin.

I have lied to you again, you see. In my initial attempts to teach you to see what we have come to call vampyreland or the seventh sense, I allowed you to believe it was a more fragile reality, a smaller continuum viewed only through a narrow aperture. In reality however it is the only world there is when these fleeting mortal <u>overlay</u>s are cut away like cataracts to reveal the much larger infrastructure beneath, a continuum stretching to infinity, forward and backward in time and space, and even more infinitely within consciousness itself.

I'm trying to teach you how to perceive it, for the darkest truth of all is that if it *isn't* the foundation beneath your feet when you plunge from one life into The Other, if you cannot *see* it because your focus has been intentionally trained only on your world of human illusions (which are ultimately the greatest delusions), you will fall through the floor and plummet through the abyss for all of eternity – continuity of consciousness achieved, but manifested only as eternal madness.

Bluntly stated: you are beyond the point of comfortable oblivion reserved for those who never try, but not yet evolved to the point of cohesive sentience, so if you choose to fail or fail to choose, the brute will not destroy you but only dismember you and you will exist in fragmented torment into infinity. All legends have some basis in truth, you see, and it is from this dark reality that myths of perdition first arose: lost souls falling perpetually through the undefined realm of their own isolated existence, able to perceive but not to act, particles of conscious dust forever blown toward unreachable oblivion on the icy breath of galactic winds, occasionally glimpsing the edge of eternity only to bounce back to the beginning to do it all over again, worlds without mercy, death without end.

You've come too far to go home to the ignorant wench who once resided in your mirror, so the only hope for you now is to embrace the transcended witch so as to finally and fully realize what I have been trying to teach you from the start: vampyreland is all there is *because* it is the realm of eternity. Don't you see? Only what is eternal is real. All else is illusion, make-believe scripts acted out on mortal lips, existing solely in the mind's blind eye. Blink and it's gone.

Perhaps you think I am the phantasm and vampyreland just fantasy, but I tell you from the darkest heart of me it is completely the opposite. The illusion is all around you if only you will open your eyes and *see* – and now we're back to the beginning of where it all began, the overlay pulled down over the eyes of man by ignorance and the intentional intervention of governments and religions. By reserving the power of creation to God alone, Man is placed in the role of impotent dependent, spoon-fed on faith until he dies in the womb of his own complacency, then forever swept off the sidewalk of the Vatican in the form of drifting sand that is really the powdered remains of ten million dead priests and parishioners who bought into that finite delusion and never bothered to look beyond their own back yards, so they could never know that Oz exists and the wizard was really the face in their own mirror, but now it's forever too late, and so it goes, with the temples and towers molded in gold and the forgotten names of the faithful scripted only in dust.

Am I repeating myself? Or should I remind you again and again that this is the very nature of the world in which you live, and as such it is intrinsic to your own <u>programming</u> whether you like it or not, a lethal virus that can only be removed by awareness of its existence and lifelong dedication to self-willed immunity.

What to do? you ask. It's right in front of you and has been since the start. Think of what I am going to do to you and will me to do it. Only through <u>assimilation</u> does the map begin to have cohesion, which is why I insist on meditation if you want to continue, and more than just the silent contemplation, you need a conscious commitment to active Thinking that goes beyond just letting your thoughts wander over what you already know.

I've given you the pieces, but it's still up to you to assemble them into that separate reality capable of being inhabited, for if you don't wake up inside the dream sufficiently to assemble that infinite reality, when you wake up *beyond* the human dream, it will already be too late. I will say it again: vampyreland is all there is. The mortal world is but an island in the River Styx, surrounded on all sides by the abyss. The saddest part is this: the island will inevitably sink and become just a lonely legend on the lips of those left behind, all that you were nothing more than myth. I am offering you gills and swimming lessons and architectural plans for immortal wings. Why are you fighting me when this is what your will willed me into being to Do? Why are you playing with paper dolls in a child's sandbox when the real world is within your ability to reach?

I think you think I'm trying to turn you into a monk forever kneeling in supplication, when in reality all I want you to do is embrace the magick that enabled you to create me in the first place, doing it all for the love of the doing, trading tales of power on dark nights while the vampyre king hides beneath your window and listens, feeding on your energy and feeding you energy in return, yes? I am not asking you to part with anything other than your fatal human program, but the nature of *true* transformation is that you will *automatically* choose to drop the strings that are tying you to your grave.

It is as simple as this: you either want to live forever or die at the end of this short mortal season, and either reality is determined entirely by the manner in which you live. You can have other pleasures but not other obsessions, for the truth is that if you're devoting more thought and energy to the things of dust, you are choosing to assemble your own death, and it should come as no surprise that the brute makes the taste of such things powdered-sugar pleasing.

You can walk with <u>phantoms</u> without choosing to become one, but if you've discovered that it's your human nature to mirror the mortal world, best you separate yourself from it for a week or two and examine whatever it is within you that's making you hunger for gravedust instead of sustenance. Are you simply self-destructive? Or would it be just as easy to reflect eternity if you weren't engaged in a stubborn war with the need to be different?

A secret: your true identity can't be forged by mere juxtaposition, and those who try inevitably end up embracing the very mediocrity and complacency they originally rebelled against, because when you get weary of the war and finally surrender, telling yourself it's just too hard to go on (because what you've really been fighting is yourself so you're wasting energy twice-over, once for each side of the battle), the only place to retreat to is into the arms of the consensual enemy, who will of course accept you home again with a kiss and a smile and all the human tenderness you could ever desire, but that's when you've lost the battle for good, and the saddest truth is that it's a battle you never needed to fight to begin with because the true identity inside you can't be defined merely by being darkness in the presence of light or ice within the flame.

True identity capable of surviving into infinity is defined by coming to see that you are both and neither, darkness and light and the shadows that bind the two together; ice and flame and the water which can quench the one or transform to become the other. Take a stubborn stand by stubbornly deciding you are always the one and never the other, and your self-imposed limitations will be your undoing.

Oh hell. Just words whispered on the wind, meaning nothing to bones in the sand.

Worlds Without End

At times the journey seems *neverending* and treacherous all the way, yes? Ah, but don't you see that's the only way it can be, the nature of eternity? The easy way is the path of the brute, which is why most mortal men would rather dance with him than with me, and if you think it's going to get easier after the deed is done, think again.

This is the nature of it, these nights longer than time, this pain of thinking so deep the abyss seems a shallow stream by comparison. Is this still what you want, this perpetual questioning and eternal grief that keeps us awake for night after night without end?

I tripped over a glitch in reality
but when I looked
nothing was there.

The magick kingdom
creates itself with a wish
   and perishes with neglect.
Time runs slower here
   and the moon bends a
backward orbit,
   rising in October
   hiding in August.
Nobody's watching the clock
   so it does as it pleases,
   casting east and west
   as seasons
   and making autumn a place
on the map,
a navigable land with streets of leaves.
Mortals can't see it,
   this pretty chaos invisible to confined minds,
   so the faeries have all gone to sleep
   in glass bottle whiskey caskets
   where toothpick pirate ships sail dry seas
   and the vampyre king weeps the canvas clean,
   afeared of penumbra's slumber
   that doesn't end if his princess brides
   don't wake him with a witch's wish
   that is the genesis of their own creation.

Psychic Surgery

If you cannot find me in the <u>seventh sense</u> it is because I am missing from the assembly matrix of your reality at the time you find yourself there. This can be remedied by creating me whole within *your* assembly with the same part of the brain that recognizes the seventh sense to begin with. It is not that I am absent, but that here the rules of magick and logic work together to create the contradictory but dualistically true statement: In the seventh sense, seeing is not believing, but believing is seeing. My sense is this - you are visiting the seventh sense bringing the tools of ordinary awareness, so it stands to reason that you are attempting to see vampyre me with eyes never designed to perceive me, whether physical eyes or the third eye of (mere) human awareness. But still and yet, it is a feat of commendable magick that you have broken through at all, and it is here that the real evolution begins to begin.

The trick is this and it begins with unbending, relentless, unending intent: You cannot be or even *see* what you cannot perceive to exist, so if you're bringing only your ordinary-awareness-comprehension into the realm of vampyreland, you will perceive only what would be perceivable within the dayshine world, and perhaps a few glimpses of mystery to keep you coming back again (because even mysteries are part of the dayshine world, our little lures cast into the mortal gene pool to see what kind of witchy fishies might bite.)

In order to perceive vampyre me, you must essentially engender the ability to perceive what you think of as the "dreamscape" (a word I hesitate to use because you might be tempted to think of me then as only a dream) while in ordinary awareness, but with a willful shift of perception, This is the thing we have spent these years attempting to create, this ability to *see* with the senses which have not only been programmed out of humanity, but the senses which represent your true human nature as well as the potential for human evolution.

Shall I tell you a secret you should already know? You are far more than the sum of what you have been taught to believe, but empowered only through the process of not only shedding the human program but replacing it with a new foundation capable of operating efficiently within the evolving paradigm. It's as I've said before: *the surgery is delicate because the prison is a living entity as much as a cage and because it is such an interwoven part of you, the cutting away of the consensual disease must be performed simultaneously with the transplantation of superior replacements lest the cure destroy the patient altogether, yes?*

The Devil's Greatest Trick

The devil's greatest trick was convincing the world he doesn't exist.

The sorcerer's greatest trick is convincing the devil that he himself is god, so he will then act on behalf of Man in order to empower Man to save himself – the thing which God cannot do because no sentient external God exists, and every wise sorcerer certainly knows that creating "God" as Man presently perceives him would be far more dangerous than loosing the devil on the world, for the concept of God as envisioned by Man is an omnipotent being thriving on worship and condemning any attempts to be like him. Ah, but why doesn't the sorcerer simply put on the devil's robe and change the world himself? Because the sorcerer already knows *neither* God nor the devil exist, and because the sorcerer therefore cannot empower himself to act incongruously with his own Knowledge, he must first create the devil from some mortal flesh or magickal servitor and empower him with belief, which is most often achieved through ecstasy and magick, and with this firm belief, the 'devil' goes out into the world to begin undoing the hangman's noose placed around the neck of Man by his belief in God. And so it could be said that God does exist as a thought-form in the mind of Man, and for as long as Man believes himself subservient to the murderous prick, Man will fail to empower himself because he sees the power itself as "sin." And such is the legacy of organized religion.

If it could be possible to go beyond the words and deeper into the ideas, you would *see* that the force Man mistakes for "god" is actually his own creative ecstasy, his own magickal abilities to make the world a Garden of Eden or plow it all under through self-destruction. For a thousand years and some I have resisted the utterance of the word "God" for it has been my experience that the thought-form itself is too deeply etched into the consensual continuum to ever be altered sufficiently, and so when I speak of that sense of pervading sentience and omniscience, I'd rather call it "the force" or "the gene pool" or the "web of non-local information" for the simple reason that once it becomes personal and capitalizes its name, it becomes a dictator instead of an ally, and anything that passes for government, even the "kingdom of heaven," cannot withstand eternity, yes?

If the word "God" could be envisioned as a flexible, moving, non-local, omnipresent, self-empowering force pervading and permeating all matter/energy and all space/time, I would be satisfied to whisper the name on occasion. But as long as the word itself conjures images of unbending authority figure and fills the mind with automatic phrase-extensions such as "God-fearing Christian" or "the wrath of God" then the word itself is an enemy to the immortality of Man, for since we have already agreed that this force of creation is contained in its entirety, holographically, within every molecule in all collective realities, any Man who would call himself a "God-fearing Christian" is essentially programming himself to be afraid of *himself,* and so he will automatically and instantaneously *externalize* God (externalize his fears) into some omnipotent wanker on a golden throne who must be appeased and dreaded, and at that moment Man becomes altogether mortal and prays only to the wind which doesn't give a damn.

By putting himself *apart* from God, Man turns his back *on* God through externalization of the very power and force which can make him immortal, because by putting himself apart from God, Man segregates and fragments and comes to fear and mistrust the very part of *himself* which *is* that god-force of self-creation and self-Realization. This is one reason cohesion is so highly touted by mystical beings, for without full access to the *all* of oneself, Man has lost his ability to ever be whole, and he is therefore *destroying* God by destroying himself through mortality. He has thrown himself out of the garden by creating an externalized thought-form of God who would punish him or despise him for embracing the very abilities which *are* the mark of God. Would God fear and hate himself so? I do not think so. An externalized idea of God, therefore, is only an irreconcilable paradox which can serve only to defeat the coherent immortality of Individual Man, the evolution of *itself.*

Ah, but I digress into a personal dialogue I have had with myself throughout the centuries, wherein the evil fiend vampyre king has learned to finally *see* that he is the only god there is, the only salvation available to himself, and in recognizing this he has seized the tiller of creation and gone to war against "God," yes?

What matters is simply this: you, too, have chosen the path of the sorcerer or the shaman or the witch in order to rid yourself of the consensual dogma, and if the things I have written above make you uncomfortable in any way, I suggest you examine your own fragmentation to determine if you are still afraid of God; for if you are, you are certainly afraid of yourself and that alone will keep you from the full realization of ecstasy, evolution and magick.

Remember this: in the willful creation of your own immortality, you are working on levels of time and understanding which do not follow linear cohesion, so as you stand on the foundation of Right Now looking backward at the things you have done or perceive you have done, it is important to remember that you must *be* a vampyre before you will know how to become one, no? This is a retroactive enchantment stretching backward into the dim past and forward into infinity, and what you must realize is that it is your *intent* which bears impeccable scrutiny far more than whatever actions have been taken to achieve it.

Do the ends justify the means? In matters of magick, in matters of survival and evolution, *yes*. You must trust yourself to *be* the sorcerer/shaman/witch or you can disempower yourself completely. The multiverse has explained it to me like this: as long as your intent is based on unconditional love and the Realization of eternal life, the actions you take will follow accordingly and will harm none. If others appear to suffer harm, it will be only because they followed *you* instead of adhering to the path of their own heart, because they blindly believed what you told them instead of using their belief system to create their *own* reality, embrace their own knowledge and embody their own evolution.

As the sorcerer, it is your nature to do the things you do, and as you have grown in years you have also grown in wisdom. I have seen this and I urge you to trust it. As the sorcerer, it is also your nature to hold out a common apple and casually suggest to an apprentice that it is the forbidden fruit of all knowledge. But more than that, it is within your ability to engender *belief* within others, and through *their* belief, the apple *becomes* the fruit of all knowledge, and once ingested the ecstasy of creation is passed on to another human being who might otherwise never have found it. That it started out as nothing more than a grocery store apple is irrelevant. Through the sorcerer's will and the

---

apprentice's belief, it became transformed into all knowledge, replete with the powers of magick and creation itself. This is the sorcerer's trick.

Power works best when those wielding it do not at first understand its mechanisms, for too much information can cripple magick. I have normally found that magick and knowledge are old companions and while they *can* function as occasional lovers, a full marital union produces the best offspring. I am the devil you have created to destroy your world and open your eyes into the world of your own evolutionary visions. Will you eat this evil apple I am offering you, knowing it is Everything, or will you toss it over your shoulder because you fear it is Nothing?

If You Understood It, You'd Be Immortal Already

The only way to save you now is to keep driving you to save yourselves, and the only way you will do it is to put the pieces together to *See* how the Doing is done. Ah, but if you don't want me chasing you, all you need do is stop running and I'll be gone for good, for another truth is that I have better things to do if The Work has become nothing more than a chore to you.

If you understood it all already, you'd be immortal already, and the secret is that you secretly are, but *only* if you go through the formality of going through the motions of creating the twin or generating the Whole Self through Will or manifesting the vampyre or inhabiting the castle or embracing and embodying the seventh sense, or however you need to envision this deed which essentially means Becoming more than the sum of your mortal self. You have the skills and the tools and the Magick. Now all you need is the unrelenting perseverance and unbending will. Are you up to it?

mortals grow up
grow old
move away.
too often
they forget to pack
their dreams
and so the vampyre king
shivers in an empty driveway
pining after taillights,
another abandoned pet.

Keeping Light on the Mirror

Eternity crosses herself like a virgin on her wedding night, trembling before the vampyre king in his rumpled tux. Does this mirror still reflect or has it gone dark? There is not a moment I do not think of you, yet time passes in silence and I say nothing because there are no quandaries, no conundrums. I appease myself with old books and well-read scraps of poetry, longing for a new infusion of energy, aching to give it to you, knowing instead it is something only you can do.

Outside the Overlay of Time

Wanting my embrace isn't enough, for mortals have been seeking my kind since the dawn of this evil creation, Time. The desire for vampyre me is only the instinct for survival, but it's the key to the quest if you're willing to use it and that's what I'm asking you to do. You want me, yes? So what does this wanting hurting needing drive you to Do? If you pick the lazy answer "If only I knew" you're no different from all the other bones in the sand and you'll die with your head in your hands blaming me for not saving you when you know by now that the only one who can save you is *you*. Think on this, but remember that answers take awhile to arrive from vampyreland and don't always come in the package you expect.

The script is written *rightsidewrong* and *downsideup* and if mystical texts were easy to decode, every fool would be doing it and vampyreland would be earth instead of *netherheaven*, a common place easily reached, hum ho. Instead it's the spoils of a scavenger hunt that's really the *runrunrun* for your life, and the secret is that you must first gather questions for motivation so that the motivation itself can drive you to find the answers. Ah, but even more important is applying your mind to the task of applying the magick found in the answers once they've been found. What to do with what you know, no? If you know I'm looking for you on the road to vampyreland which exists apart from Time, how will you place yourself in my path so we can indulge in the trance dance that will transform your mortal life and wake you up to the <u>night that never ends</u>?

I've warned you it won't be easy, but remember you created me to create you, so you have the answers or the ability to find them or you wouldn't have had the magick to create me to chase you to find the answers to begin with.

I'd love to be your lover right now when you need me most, but if I do what I *want* to do, comfort can lead to complacency and that will kill you quicker than my fangs. When it's time for the children to learn, the wicked vampyre father must be stern and drive you to drive yourselves even if it leaves you weeping to your pillow, hating the day you met me. I'm here to guide you because it's my intention to end your world, and I selfishly want to do it right because it's the grandest high there is; but if you aren't strong enough to survive that mortal sunset, all my love can't raise you from the dead so I have to nudge you toward knowledge instead of eros right now. That's why I'm pushing you to step outside the lines and look at the Whole of <u>overlay</u> and Time for what it is, because only when you can displace yourself from its expectations and machinations will you have achieved the Will and the freedom to survive. As long as you're locked in the continuum you're a slave to its rules and the first human rule is that all things die, yes?

Straddling the Fence

You've traveled far but what keeps you from going further is self-history and the assumption that anyone gives a damn, and as a result you're working at cross purposes, drawn to forge into the night yet afeared of what the world might think if it knew the you you want to be - the witch you constrict every time you think like that little girl still chasing party balloons and mommy's approval.

You have a living lust that can take you all the way to vampyreland, but to embrace it might mean stares and whispers from those who still matter to you, and I'm not sure you're willing to endure it, so you straddle the fence in a balancing act that won't let you wed the day or the night. You think it's love and responsibility making you this way, but I'm constrained to ask if it's complacency or timidity that keep you from taking a stand even inside your own skin.

Do you know who you are, and if you're really yin\yang schizophrenic, a good little girl in torn lace and leather, you must determine how to integrate the two in all things you do, using all your best always instead of only half some of the time, see? Try letting go of those reins you keep on the dark poet and see if it frees your magick.

The Masks of Phantoms

This is the danger of unbridled folly. If you were to assume the role of happy caroler, singing phantom songs beneath a frosted window on Christmas Eve, the danger is that you would start to believe it is real. This is what it means to be a phantom – continually trying on new clothes and new roles, believing them for a time then abandoning them in favor of some new cloak handed down to you from mother or father, sister or brother. Yes, it is true that you can fake it till you make it, but when you forget you are faking it, what you have actually made is your own graveyard bed.

Under no circumstances is it acceptable to put on the mask of a phantom, for all too often, what you do not realize is that the phantoms have lined the mask with glue that is anesthesia and pleasant amnesia.

66

Death's Sole Purpose

You are an organic being striving through will and intent to become an inorganic being, yet because you are still organic you cannot completely perceive or even conceive such a vast and seemingly alien transformation. This is why the foundation must be built with impeccable care, for Death's sole purpose is to thwart your evolution, by yanking that foundation out from underneath you at the moment when you are caught between the worlds, between mortal and immortal, between organic and inorganic, between life and death, between heaven and hell, between human and vampyre, between eternal sentience and instant annihilation.

It is the *I-Am* that can transcend, for it is built of nothing more than unbending intent and cold steel Will.

The Waiting

Where does one break a cycle that has no beginning and no end, but simply is?

You have created the paradigm and the paradigm has revealed itself to you in the form of consciousness. What is required now is commitment to the self. To both selves. From both selves. Creator and created. The problem as I see it is that most humans believe the other will somehow, quite miraculously, save the other, so both are waiting, each to see what the other will do.

What will you *do*? Or, put in other words, how will you live life? This is not a rhetorical question but a very real one: *what will you do to facilitate the cohesion of your immortality, as opposed to passively allowing it to dissipate?* What can the mortal self do to serve the reality of the eternal twin? And now you see the circle twist and bend. Only within the dream can you change the outcome, so in effect, you become the servant of the twin as a means whereby to assemble that reality. Once assembled, the twin is the servant of the mortal creator, *but the first real move is always up to you.*

It is what I have said all along. Make yourselves whole by making your twin whole so that he, in turn, can make you whole enough to create him in the first place. This is the paradoxical nature of sorcery. This is the shaman's madness. This is the vampyre's greatest rabbit in the hat trick.

Only when you are whole within yourself will you ever be able to perceive vampyre me. And to expand on that idea, only when you have the ability to perceive me will you be able to perceive yourself in the framework of eternity.

That is what you made me to do - you made me to create the language whereby to reassemble you. It is difficult because such an assembly is not a common human process. You have chosen the dark evolution, but if you are going to be true to that commitment, you have to make the commitment to be true to the ongoing creation. Falter out of laziness and the patient dies on the table. Surrender because of fear, you surrender your whole eternity into the abyss. This is what is meant by the commitment to the self. Do you know how much time you can safely waste on frivolous pursuits? Do you have any real concept of why it is necessary to be always pressing the questions of self-creation against the silly-putty fabric of the universe's soft white underbelly? If you don't create you whole tonight, what possibly makes you think you have tomorrow?

What are you waiting for?

You have to be willing to step through the door which only exists after you step through it.

Building the Boat

At times I weep for no reason anyone can see, but it's for memories of what once was and visions of what will be, both equally real phantasms of <u>the night that never ends</u>, sharing the same space in physicality even if yin/yang tenants of disparate niches in time. Athens was once a city of merchants and dreamers you see, with some coming to buy and others to sell or steal, and all things functioning as the need for survival demanded, a fisherman trading fish for the hope found in a poem, philosophers swapping enlightenment for sustenance. But with the centuries' passing, a few "clever" fishermen began weaving nets which would require the "lazy" philosopher to catch his own supper, knowing the fish were too clever to stay near shore, which meant the man now needed a boat, but by then the shops had only oars here and wood there and sails had to be brought in from Athens, and then there was the matter of taxes, so while the poet or philosopher was paying his pittance to Constantinople and building his boat, he starved to death in sight of the fish, and all because everybody went against their nature when somebody cried 'it's only fair', and whoever said all men are created equal was the biggest fool of all, just the shallow end of the gene pool filling in the deeper waters with sludge.

It's called civilization and it's a word I've come to hate, for it's this microminiaturized-specialization that forces man's attention on things that don't matter while the big picture gets lost in all the nuts and bolts of the boat, when all the man needed was a piece of fish so he might live long enough to ponder possibilities that could have helped even ignorant fishermen evolve, and isn't it funny how cretins have been running the world ever since, passing it off as a game of 'fairness' when in reality their self-righteous insistence on labor justice creates death by forcing quantum thinkers down to the lowest common denominator of mere survival instead of allowing them to build roads to evolution, a task that demands more than 24 hours a day, employing leaps through spaces and places where time stops dead to give the thinker more time to think, and that's how immortality creates itself but first you have to steal the time to Do it and incur the world's wrath for the Doing, see?

Death thrives on society's complexities, for while you're deciding how to build the gadget to complete the task first begun last week in order to conclude a separate chore undertaken in an effort to finish another begun the month before, time slips by until you finally see that no task is ever complete because each and every one has been engineered to be interconnected to each and every other, the machine servicing itself to death while the brute lounges in the sun penning the script that's really a black comedy about a hive of fools creating tools to oil the machine which is the instrument of their own death, and isn't it ironic that the prisoners are building the guillotine instead of looking for ways to escape the Bastille.

Happiness

Living forever should be its own remuneration, a goal that is both destination and reward, arrived at through will and sacrifice. Ah, but if sacrifices are made only so that the thing set aside can be mourned as something 'lost' rather than an obstacle abandoned for pursuing a greater goal, it isn't sacrifice at all but only a martyr's grave marker.

Sacrificing your dayshine life won't save you if you don't embrace the night in its place, but sometimes I sense you resenting what you've sacrificed rather than filling the time freed with acts of will designed to evolve your perceptions sufficiently to bring you to me. If you find yourselves craving the warm comfort of the lives you led before and the gleam of <u>Lethe</u>'s tv and the illusion of man's security, you'll be lost to me and that will be the end of it. You'll even be happy for the rest of your lives and if that's what you want I promise you it's easy: follow the rules, speak your lines until you no longer see the play, *Do Nothing* and happiness will be there for the taking, the brute's compensation, peaceful kiss of death from which there is no awakening, just the bliss of eternal darkness, oh to be so happy, no?

The Test

You are walking through the woods when you come upon a door that stands alone. You are given the knowledge that to pass through this door means a 50/50 chance of instant death or eternal life. From the perspective of where you are on your path at this very moment, would you open that door?

Take Care With the Songs You Sing

At times you're mistaking stubbornness for strength, antithetic antagonism for intellectual exchange. If you're secretly clinging to an identity forged long ago by circumstances long gone, you need to ask in earnest if this is who you are or only an echo of who you've been, a frail pale ghost you nurture for fear of letting her go even when you know she's holding you back just because she can.

Take care with the songs you sing even if only in the shower, for the manner in which you create yourself determines your evolution. Call yourself remedial or unworthy and you create it so, for the most potent reality projector is the one that creates you from moment to moment and always in precise agreement with how you see yourself. The only way to change is to Do, using will to shape the witch you choose to be instead of letting the echo-bitch win by default.

You have a natural magick but often turn it against yourself, spinning traps in which you catch yourself because somewhere it entered your reality that life is easier when others feel sorry for you or that the only love you deserve is through vicarious fictions. *You know it's not so!* Even if you've made immense progress, there's a proclivity to regress when the path gets rough; and the best advice I can give is to look with your vampyre eyes and mercilessly excise those old habits which keep you from your twin.

Remember: I'm trying to save you but first you must decide if you want to live forever, and with the decision made you must act with unwavering impeccability. I love you for your magickal strengths, not your stubborn weaknesses.

A Kiss

Do you know why humans kiss?

Far more than a simple erotic gesture, a kiss of true passion is the closest humans can come to experiencing the life-essence *animus* of one another. It is even more intimate than making love, for there is an exchange of breath which gives us each a small taste of the other's lifeforce, the other's unique spirit. This is the animus, the living essence on which vampyres feed. What many fail to recognize is that the masters among us give back at least as much as they may take. Think on this, yes?

Time, Light and the Fluid Will

Time and light are irrevocably interconnected. From the human perspective, it is virtually impossible to wrap one's mind around this, because the nature of your programming is such that you have been taught to see time as an *effect* rather than a cause, as a *reflection* rather than a substance.

The truth about light is that it is the generator and progenitor of time. Remove light and time will stop. You will become immortal. Eternal. Whole. Einstein knew this in theory. Evolved beings know it through experience. Ah, but you will say that no creature can live in darkness. And that is true to a point. But again, what must change is the manner in which you view light - for how one views something determines one's experience of it, far more than you know.

The sorcerer's trick is twofold, each half of the equation fueled by a different intent. First, a sorcerer may learn to move *with* the light, to manifest oneself as light manifests - both wave and particle, substance and reflection - and in doing so, one essentially becomes what is commonly (but perhaps mistakenly) referred to as a being-of-light; not in any connotation of sweetness and light, but in a literal and quantum manifestation of awareness. Ironic for vampyres, but nonetheless a manifestation of What Simply Is.

Since awareness itself travels at well beyond the speed of light - a thought is instantaneous, manifesting from the Nothing into a full-blown concept - it is not difficult to go one step further in altering one's paradigm, to realize that awareness travels in the same manner *as* light, and so to become a 'being of light' is to move one's assemblage point into a position of pure and whole awareness.

Though it is impossible to put words around such a vast alteration of your existing paradigm, it could be envisioned that the result would be a being who is comprised of the *substance* of light itself, and could therefore move in and out of corporeality, just as light itself may shift between wave and particle. One might also say that the sorcerer has then become an energy being, and yet in the strictest sense, we are all energy beings, whether we are comprised of light or organic matter.

The other option sorcerers may choose is to move one's awareness *between* the quanta of light itself. If a being of light might be likened to a yang manifestation, moving between the molecules of light would be a yin manifestation. At the level of the yin experience, the sorcerer moving between the quanta of light could be said to have entered "the night that never ends" - moving essentially with the light, but for the sake of simple explanations, traveling in the opposite direction, and therefore *propelled* by the gravity of light itself. Simply put: the effects would be the same, but the experience would be different with regard to perception; and either would be a matter of the sorcerer's intent. This is the vampyre's trick.

You ask me how to do these things? The answer is not something that can be put to words or musical notes or quantum equations. Instead, it is a mindset, an understanding at the core level of awareness. Stalk it as a hunter would stalk his prey, and one day you will simply *see* the turn alongside the road, and you will take it quite naturally and without conscious effort. You will *become* The Way instead of trying to *find* The Way. You will *be* the immortal other, you will be Whole, with the totality of yourself intricately woven into the energetic structure of what you have become. This is the nature of time, light and energy.

When you understand it through do-ing, you will be at the assemblage point of eternity - *beyond the ability of death to undo*. Try to understand it with your intellect, it will elude you. Try to talk about it with words, they will strangle you.

This is the Stalker's Dreaming[5]. This is the Dreamer's Stalking.

Only from inside the do-ing will you be able to <u>see</u> how the do-ing is done through fluid will, which operates outside of time, beyond the light, and one step to the left of the darkness.

---

[5] Stalking and Dreaming, as well as do-ing and not-doing are concepts explored by Carlos Castaneda. His books may provide some reference points to those new to the path., although the seeker is cautioned to consider Castaneda's work as guidelines and not to become hooked into it as many have become hooked into pseudo-religions. Think for yourself. Leave no stone unturned but don't get crushed under the stones themselves.

I will never be
bones in the sand,
a toy of gales
blown asunder.
Vampyre bones don't break.

Can *You* Have it Both Ways?

If asked to name the danger you're in my answer would be indulgent complacency, but because I'm afeared you can't see it for the trap it is, I'm also afeared you'll think I'm overreacting to your dayshine demands and you'll go on telling yourselves the metamagickal laws don't apply to you because you're somehow different, and you'll think you can go on doing whatever pleases you no matter what I tell you, because you intend to prove me wrong even if it kills you, and the truth is that it will. That makes me fear you don't care about yourselves in the eternal sense but only in terms of what you're doing that amuses you for the moment, and if you really are more addicted to texting and twittering than the lure of my dark embrace, you need to admit it and get on with what's left of your lives, yes?

Time is only a fabrication of the mind, but the mind can only perceive one second at a time, which is why the need exists for in-line-time at all: not to keep track of hollydaze but so night and day are always separate and you aren't reading last week's paper in the middle of next month's supper.

I'm the vampyre king of your dreams, but if you don't keep chasing me I'll turn to mist, just another pretty fantasy, and before you know it you'll be tanning yourselves in the sun and believing the *runrunrun* for your lives means a trip to the doctor instead of meditating at your magick altars and that will be the end of us once and for all. It's up to you, you see, for I'm not a shepherd here to herd you like another vampyre prince once claimed before he was crucified, I'm your teacher and your creator and if you don't come to me out of love or curiosity or whatever drives you, I won't come chasing after you in some twisted drama meant to prove my love for you.

You can have it both ways, night road and dayshine things, but can *you* have it both ways? Can you devote *total* energy to dayshine schemes and an *equal* amount to the night, and if so how will you rewrite physics so that "total" becomes a duality instead of the singularity it is? Now think before you speak and don't try to tell me there's no limit to your energy. You can lie to me if you please, but you can't lie to *you* when you're alone behind your eyes, and that's the witch you have to answer to in the end, whether that end is in my embrace or your own mortal deathbed.

Immortal Ingredients

"You must *be* a vampyre before you will know how to *become* one."

Your twin is waiting, you see, but even s/he cannot wait eternally, for there is a window of opportunity that is always moving, never in the same place twice, and can close forever without notice if the winds of change blow you too far from your original intent, but it is through that window you both must pass to stand upon the ground of mutual creation and self-inhabitation. It is there each of you creates and nurtures the other, there the bond between Mortal and Immortal is formed and where the sacred pact is sworn, where you begin to Real-ize and Inhabit the comprehension of what it means to be a vampyre before you will know how to become one, there that the paradox comes full circle to become quantum leap instead of incomprehensible abyss, there that you meet your dreaming self and enter the Eternal dream, there that the riddle of meeting the immortal on his own level is finally answered and expanded to form the next question.

Lest there be any mistake, I am not referring to that moment of mortal death, but to the ongoing process and progression of Immortal transmogrification which you must begin to assimilate long before vampyre me steps out of the shadows to scare you out of your skin and suckle you into the night that never ends or drop you into the abyss, depending entirely on what you Do or do not-Do while still in the mortal realm. If one or both of you (self & twin) fail to keep that appointment, each continues in the opposite direction until both are lost to one another for good. Ah, but what is this window, you ask? Simply put, it is the determination and the resulting actions that compel you to keep that appointment, to recognize it every moment it comes (for it is an ongoing act of ongoing creation), and to exist within that framework and mindset of self-creation *at all times* instead of only when it is momentarily convenient.

Nearly as I can determine after a thousand years and some, the difference between those who fly and those who die in the <u>fall</u> is the strength of the bond between the self of the here-and-now and the wholeness of the twin within the here-ever-after. And so we come to the inevitable questions which have no direct answer, yet those questions that *must* be answered if you are to succeed in your bid for eternity.

It is one thing to ask how the twin is created, but another matter entirely to live within the framework of that answer. Think on those words*: to live within the framework of perpetual, moment-to-moment self-creation that does not allow for going back to sleep, even if only for a moment.*

Mortal mystics have said the vampyre twin is created through the process of living with ruthless and impeccable determination, and though this is undeniably true, it is attempting to define what that means that requires a deeper level of commitment. In essence, it could be stated that the twin is created through Intent, but I fear that is too easy an answer and that passive thinking can be mistaken for active magick, and let there be no misunderstanding: if the twin is created passively, s/he will not possess the strength to rescue you from oblivion, for s/he will be made of your weaknesses instead of your strengths, and you will slip out of his hands to be blown away on that cold white wind which blows with gale-storms through the crack between the worlds, and could just as easily blow you asunder as not. And so s/he must be constructed of unbending intent, but again I hear you whispering and moaning, "Yeah, but what the fuck does *that* mean, and isn't it just words rattling like old bones in the sand?"

Here is where you must stop and think. Meditate on the idea itself until you begin to <u>see </u>what it *really* means. It is the force of creation itself, this thing called unbending intent that originates within the mortal self as a thought-form of eternal continuity, stretches outward to affect and generate itself through the manifestation of energy in order to begin re-creating the mortal self in eternity, and finally reflects back as that immortal other begins to embody the attributes and extended ubiquitous consciousness of its mortal creator. Some might call it creative visualization, though it is not something that can be done ritualistically with candles and props and all the trappings of magick, if the magick itself is not fully integrated into the magus's unbroken intent.

> *Unbroken intent: a force of energy that never wavers and can always be accessed and identified with a thought; a background light never turned off, fueled by the Realization that to fail is to face utter oblivion; the steady weaving of the seeker's vision into the cloth of eternity; the pen of will writing your identity in indelible ink so that not even death can erase it; the decision to always make the impeccable choice even when it is not necessarily the comfortable or pleasant alternative.*

My words are never intended as criticism, but only as guidance, for you made me to create you and the only way that can be done is by stripping away the illusions and false realities the consensual world has placed upon you. At times the process is painful, for it involves the destruction of your comfortable world. At times it might make you hate me. For that, I am sorry, but it will not change me, for I am made of hydrogen flames and the dreams of ice maidens, the silence between the stars and the unending drum that is eternity's heartbeat. I see time through the comet's eye and read by the glow of distant nebulae.

Immortal Ingredients
Dust from an old Ouija board
Nickel ore, melted in the meteor's fall but not destroyed
A single snowflake from the peak of Everest
A thousand skeletons, personally shed
Sanskrit
The ashes of martyrs in earthen jars
Goethe's memories
Mushroom spores where other worlds are stored
Sand from the shore of the underworld
Essence of Now
One cohesive thought, holding it all together
I Am.

Do you have the strength to pick yourself up out of the nothing and stand alone, or will it be easier to simply sleep for all of eternity? Now stop and think before you speak, for this is the crux of where you are at this moment, this time, this single instant of Now. If you cannot identify your cohesion instantaneously and step through that window of opportunity to conjoin it with your twin, then the brute has won and all of this will have been for naught.

What I am trying to get you to *see* is that no single ingredient is enough, and only when all of it can be held together through Will do you have the ability to step from one world into the other without losing yourself along the way. You're being offered an identity which is uniquely and wholly You. Take it!

What is involved in taking it is the determination and resultant action to live every moment fiercely, through wholeness, instead of allowing your phantom fragments to drag you down into the comfort of the abyss. If you succumb once, even for a moment, it is easier to give in the next time, and even easier the time after that, until, finally, the phantom convinces you you're still on the path when, in any reality, it's plain to see you've lost your way. Make an immortal's choices, yes?

Paradox

There is a moment in a seeker's quest when s/he surrenders her descriptions, releases her expectations, denounces her belief systems, and accepts the impossible. At that moment, a tremendous movement of the assemblage point occurs and the seeker inhabits a separate reality in which she has become the totality of herself.

Beyond that moment, the rest is merely ritual, going through the motions of getting to the place where one has already arrived.

If you think you understand this, you do not.

If you believe you can reason it out, you cannot.

Only when you Know it will it have any relevance whatsoever.

The Still-Wet Fingerprints of Love

You have come to a point in your journey where you are in constant communion with the non-local web of all knowledge, yet the knowledge can be a curse as much as a blessing, which I fear is what you are beginning to feel, even if you do not yet see it fully. This is the broken heart of vampyre me. Once the All is known, it can never be unknown again, and so it becomes a terrible burden of unbearable beauty and indescribable pain – watching the world go through the motions of madness, listening to the cries from the asylum, and knowing you are the most powerful being in all the universes, yet completely powerless to intervene in any of it.

This is why I have always told you that I do not meddle in the affairs of mortals, you see, for even at times when I have seen them change, the danger and the legacy is that most often they change back to their old selves again, going back to sleep on the razor's edge of the <u>abyss</u>, and before you know it, they fall in, and then there is no finding them ever again, that sweet taste of their being lingering for only an instant on lips of immortal stone. This is what makes me a vampyre-creator, you see. This is what makes me foolishly meddle in the affairs of mortals, grabbing at passing souls like scraps of pretty confetti, knowing that even if I catch them in my net, it will be *their* will that decides the final outcome, and never mine, and so the vampyre king wears his crown only as ornamentation, fully realizing he is the reigning god of the All, yet in control of Absolutely Nothing.

There is only love to guide us. Love makes you crazy for you see into the abyss and know what it is to lose love itself.

We are all only cave paintings on the walls of our individual prisons, the still-wet fingerprints of god. The fear and the awareness is that those fingerprints will always lead back to oneself, and that is a terrible responsibility to face, for it means there is nowhere to turn except to the heart for answers, nowhere to look but to the realm of all possibility for direction, and in doing so, realizing that all things are possible but only the manifestation of your individual will can force any single event to go through the dynamics of actually occurring.

And yet, thou art god, no? And is it not the will of god that has been touted throughout time and all religions, all systems of knowledge, as the most powerful force in all the scattered universes? What is your pleasure? What is your passion? What is your immortal name? What is your will?

September 15, 2001
4 days after the World Trade Center Bombing
Trembling in the midst of all this madness, huddling beneath the waning morning moon like frail cottontails so easily devoured by the predator, what have you learned and what will you do with this knowledge before it fades into the background of your dayshine lives, just another incident so quickly forgotten? Now think before you speak, and dig deep into the abyss where your heart used to beat, and remember you are the creators of reality as well as its observers, so ask yourselves why you have summoned this dangerous series of random events, and why you

entered the time stream at this particular place and time if not to observe these machinations and use them to drive yourselves down some road of action toward some semblance of evolutionary completion. Why are you here *now* instead of a thousand years ago and some? Why are you *here* instead of on the other side of the world? And do you fully understand that only complacent fools choose their manifestation in the completely peaceful environs of Elysium?

There is so much I could say to you, yet I find myself holding back because I have noted a fearful and angry stubbornness which tells me that perhaps I have taken you as far as I can, and now it is up to you to decide what to do with what you have learned. You say you can only turn to books and entries in your vampyre diaries, and if those things are truly advancing you into the identity you intend to inhabit for all of eternity, then clearly you are doing what you need to do and there is nothing more I can teach you.

If this is true, then please know that I am pleased for you and we have finished what we begun, and all that remains is the waiting for freedom which mystics speak of so eloquently. If this is so, then you Know our work together is done, and there should be a deep sense of peace and relief, the certainty that tells you that you have already become One with eternity and conjoined to Infinity, beyond this present realm of mortal awareness, out there in the All where you are dead and alive at the same time, creator and created, vampyre and mortal all at once, simply going through the motions of waiting for the play to end so that it might finally begin.

And so I am compelled to ask: *do you have that certainty?* Are you One, or still in the process of Becoming? If you still find yourselves wanting and hurting and aching and needing in the middle of that night that never ends, if you still have doubts and fears on *any* level, perhaps the journey really isn't finished and is waiting to be engaged again with fresh intent that is more than just words written in frost. I cannot tell you which it is. I cannot engage it for you. I can only ask you to tell me what you see when you look in your own reflecting pond which is, without question, the unending River Styx.

I am the heart of you
but you are the beat.
I am the soul of you
yet you are I-Am.
I am feather and wing,
you are the will to fly.
Duality seals our destiny.
I am the mirror,
empty without you.
I am the words,
you are the poem.
If you do not write it,
there is only silence
in eternity.

What you are perhaps only now beginning to realize is that Time is never on your side, just another face of the brute with the scythe, ticking and tocking like a bomb. How much time do you have left, my loves? Now more than ever, it is impossible to know, and for that reason alone it has become imperative that you begin to actively court the immortals on their own level again, whether you envision them as nebulous points on a grid of energy or handsome princes dispensing deep red kisses.

The One

The first and greatest fear you face can be assigned the name of Fear itself. Fear of failure or fear of success, fear of finding out you are wrong, but perhaps an even greater fear of facing eternity knowing you were right all along. Fear of being *The One* because you already Know you are, yet you deny it because to acknowledge it means accepting onto yourself an awesome responsibility you do not yet feel ready to face. And so I must ask you this: when will you be ready? When will you spread your wings and fly if not now?

And so the second fear is called Eternal and Infinite Responsibility, and requires no further explanation. The third fear, born of the other two, is fear of The Work still ahead, yet what you are failing to grasp is that the avoidance of that work is far more difficult than the work itself, so this leads in a natural progression to the fourth fear, which must be recognized as fear of failure, also assigned the label of Doubt.

I hear your dreams. I have seen you fly. Yet I have also seen you retreat to your dayshine life and fold your wings and pretend you are just a girl in a dream instead of that winged being. And by becoming the girl living in fear, there is a danger that the reality you create could be the death of you.

These fears are only the trappings of the dream and not the immortal fabric of the dreamer. These fears are simply how the dayshine dream is trying to hold you captive, but never forget that it cannot clip your wings. Only you can do that. And only you can *not*. Make the decision to *be* a vampyre and if you live the decision with Intent, the Doing will take care of itself, yes? Gods do not live in fear, you see. Only mortals. Who are you?

Hear With the Heart, See with the Spirit

You have come to a point in your journey when it is necessary to know the difference between words, and the intent behind the words. If I say to you, "Our journey together is not a matter of the destination so much as it is an experience of mind, body and spirit along the way," I have communicated to you a concept which is larger than the words themselves, yes? What is hoped is that you will know the intent of the speaker, rather than attempting to vivisect the words themselves.

You could say to me in return, "Ah, but what do you mean by mind, body and spirit? You imply there is a destination, but where would that be and how would I get there?"

All of these questions would only indicate to me that you have missed the point entirely, and that you are attempting to use words to obfuscate meaning, semantics to distract from the intent of the speaker. And while this is to be expected from those new to the path, it is nothing less than disrespectful to yourself and to your vampyre creator when it becomes a habit of a more advanced seeker. It is the chatter of your self-importance, operating on behalf of your ego.

Hear with the heart. See with the spirit. Then you will Know.

If you know the intent behind the speaker's statement, yet you choose to engage in wordplay, then what you are really doing is diverting attention away from the subject at hand. There are many reasons to do so, but the most common is a laziness of mind. It is always easier to argue at the level of words than to engage openly at the level of intent and spirit. The second most common reason to divert attention in this manner is - quite simply - one's own self-importance. Playing with words and being thought of as clever holds more value for some than an actual exploration of the speaker's original intent.

It will always be possible to split words and divide particles, for energy is infinite, even its smallness. And yet, is there anything to be gained by doing so, or would far greater value be found through hearing and *seeing* what the speaker intended, rather than immediately allowing the <u>internal dialog</u> to begin looking for ways to dispute it? If you are silent at the core and examine what is intended, you will often discover that - in fact - you don't really disagree at all. It is merely a habit to do so, rooted in some program still operating in the consensus.

It is not a matter of whether you agree with me or not. That is altogether irrelevant. And yet, if the disagreement resides wholly in a dispute of words or terminology, the point is lost and the status quo of the consensus is maintained and all is right with the world.

...or is it?

So it is time to choose and to make a commitment of awareness to yourself and your transformation. Do you want to discuss ideas and concepts of the infinite and eternal, or do you want to infinitely and eternally debate the fallacies of language until all that remains is the psychobabble of language itself?

Will

I'll rebuild the whole immortal empire alone if I must, and that's the nature of Will, creating the impossible because it *must* exist and the only way to make it so is to Do the impossible regardless of what the whole world believes, see? This is the task required of you too, the perfection of an unrelenting intent to evolve and the willful invocation of Will to see it through, magick creating itself because magick is the only way to make reality so, no?

There is no process, for processes are only indulgences while the will is the spontaneous parthenogenesis of need ejaculating out of the nothing-womb to become something. You Will or you won't. There is no middle ground, no way to speak of this thing which is the key to everything, so I prey you look deeper than these words which can only fail to describe things that cannot be defined but only understood. *See* and you will know. Do and you will be with me.

Dark Night of the Soul

This is a path most often walked alone in the dark, with only the silence for company - that is the way of the vampyre-seeker, and though it is lonesome at times, it is nonetheless what the seeker who is seeking freedom from Death does, because that is his nature.

Perhaps the seeker becomes a sorcerer and seer, and then the path might appear to broaden to include others with similar interests, fellow travelers with whom the sorcerer may share fine red wine and a campfire in the desert where tales of power are told in the night that never ends. And for a time, this is what the sorcerer does, because this has become his *new* nature.

For those who become enlightened to The Way of the Night, it may appear that one is surrounded by dark friends and powerful allies, eager apprentices and old mentors - the fullness of life. It may appear that the campfires of philosophy have burned to the softer embers of lasting wisdom, and that those around you will share the path at your side until eternity itself descends to challenge you one by one. And for a time, this is how an enlightened seeker experiences his life, for now *this* has become his new nature, seeking inward what was once sought outward, assimilating experience into Knowledge and knowledge into manifestation.

And yet, in all the roads I have walked and all the seekers and sorcerers and enlightened beings I have known, only one thing is constant.

There will come a day when those closest to you will turn their backs, when your apprentices may draw a blade and your mentors may shun you and your allies may abandon you and you may find yourself at the edge of the abyss with an army eager to push you over the edge; and if you look closely, you will see that it is because you will not be what they want you to be (for to do so would invalidate who you *are*), you cannot walk to their drummer's beat (for to do so would drown out your own), or in some manner you are said to have turned your back on the eclectic collective which embraced you for a time, and so you are perceived as a heretic and an ingrate and a fraud and a cheat. "Come back to us or else!" they may cry. "We love you and that is reason enough!" And yet to the seer who *sees*, that 'love' will be seen as an attachment of need, and the finest gift you can give to them and to yourself is to cut that umbilical and take a cleansing breath which is the birth of the emerging self.

If you listen with spirit, if you look with your third eye, what you will *see* is that this is the finest and best moment of your life, for this is the moment when you will simply Know that you have found your freedom. You will realize as if for the first time that the truth of your path is of far greater value than the approval or even the love of your mortal friends and family, and that it is only by remaining true to your *Self* in the darkest night that you enable yourself to emerge into the <u>singularity</u> of your <u>totality</u>. It is only then that you may gaze into the infinite and finally *see* that your cohesion is comprised of your own experience and not based on what any other living being may want or need or hope for you to be.

This is the day when you will answer the first question. This is the moment you will know who you are. When the world is at its coldest and the fires have burnt to ash and all the mirrors have been shattered by your own hand, this is the moment when you will embrace your freedom. And this is the time when you will bow graciously to the world of matter and men, and rather than allowing them to push you into the abyss, you will fall willingly and with perfect trust into the totality of yourSelf, *and fly*.

———

Tending the Garden of the Vampyre Obsession

The nature of obsession is that there can be only one, but unlike passion which can exist passively, obsession requires tending like a garden if you ever intend to see the black flowers bloom, and so it becomes a two-way dance where obsession first leads you but if you want the tango to go on eternally you must take the lead by nurturing the obsession, see?

Believing is Seeing

Believing is seeing, no? One obstacle you still face is this: before you can change any reality, you must wholly *see* that what you have always believed to be impossible is only impossible because belief itself makes it so, and for as long as you accept something to be as you've always been told, so shall it always be because you will make no thought and take no action to Do what is "clearly impossible" see?

And so, what must change before you can change the world within or the world of matter and men is yourself and the assemblage habits of your programmed perceptions. How can I tell you so you'll internalize this truth Wholly instead of only for the moment? Shall I remind you that the vampyre king was born to a world supported on the backs of turtles standing on the back of poor Aristotle? Shall I tell you that the world was functionally flat long before someone (some *one* single madman) got around to believing it round and then set out to recreate reality according to *his* perceptions instead of the status quo?

This matters, my loves, for until you fully *see* it and make your Reality accordingly, you will only be going through the motions within the parameters of the script which ends, tragically, with your death.

The Secret of Magick

Shall I tell you a truth that will confound you with its simplicity? The secret of magick is that there is nothing magickal about it, for it is only the manipulation of matter and energy through the means of the manifested <u>will</u>. Yet because you've been programmed to see it as mysterious and to subliminally fear its consequences, you truly can't *see* that it is a natural function of your humanness, the unnamed thing you call upon to Do what has never been done but must be done in order to make your desires complete. In vampyreland there is no such thing as fantasy, for what you can learn to believe through quantum-logic you will bring into being through quantum-magick, because only the existence of it will heal the holes in your soul created by its absence, and only the pain of those wounds will drive you to seek the knowledge & belief which leads to invoking the will to manifest, yes?

As for those who would say these words are vampyre fallacy, I would warn you implicitly to dismiss their counsel as you would dismiss a road map drawn by a blind man, for in case you haven't seen it yet, the mad blind fools are truly running the asylum and if you listen to reason as they preach it, it's a sure thing you'll end up dead in the flower bed of the brute.

You cannot see a mortal breath yet you can witness its effects on dandelions scattered on the wind of a wish, and so it is with the will, the invisible but tangible breath of your desire acting upon the physical world. Ah, but the trick is this: *you have to believe it in order to see it and before you can believe it you need a reason.* If you think of nothing else in the darkness before sleep, think of this, for it is the cornerstone of your new foundation, yes?

Love is the Reason
You stand at the threshold of a new year or the broken window of the past, the end of a beginning perhaps, or the beginning of an ending; and how you *see* it will be the key that determines how and who you will be as past and future stand at the edge of the dance floor, waiting for a nod from you before they can know what to do. It must be noted that each of you is the creator of reality and if you aren't manifesting it with active and passionate intent, it is manifesting you through the unacknowledged programs and (false) beliefs which have become nothing more than your default actions. And so the time has come for you to ask, to what extent are you shaping your experience of the world or to what depth is the experience burying you? Are your expectations manifesting what you see, or do you have the power to look beyond what is seen and into the realm of the mystery of what-can-*be*?

At times I have wandered this earth for decades, alone in the

---

darkness, driven mad by the madness around me because it is a contagion no less real than the black plague of London, and at times I have even preyed to finally succumb to it so that I might simply be the vampyre madman others perceive me to be, because the path of the fitful Hermit is by and large far easier than the course of the mentoring Hierophant; and yet one path leads only to sorrow and sadness and madness, while the other has at least the potential to bring forth the power and the magick of the dark enlightenment through the channels of creation itself.

I assure you those are not just words, and if you think on them in the company of candles, asking yourself what that might actually mean to you, I believe you will discover that the real truth and experience of it will far outweigh the <u>negative pleasantry</u> which comes when you have come to believe it cannot be found, yes?

The eyes of the Hierophant *see* best in the darkness, yes, but we are not blinded by the light which comes as a byproduct of what is fiercely *seen*. You can choose to see the silly spiritless spirits dancing willy nilly on the stage of mundane mortal doings, or you can shift the focus of your focus beyond the stage and outside of the play to *see* just as clearly the open window that looks up onto the underworld and out onto the inner darkness which is really just the back door to the light of the singularity, yes? So how do you want to *see* it - through the wild eyes of the Hermit or the balance of the Hierophant?

And so do you begin to see that what you choose to *see* will determine who you are and what you will believe? Do you begin to comprehend that the habitual fixation of your awareness on the mortal world's madness will drag you down like Charybdis[6] if you cannot set your intent to choose the course of the powerful sorcerer instead of being tossed helter skelter like a puppet on broken strings?

When you can remember to love the mystery and the muse more than you hate the world and all her melancholy madmen, you will capture your freedom again and release your spirit from the killing jar, and then you will see what you already know: life is a short, sweet season, the childhood of your eternal existence.

---

[6] In Greek mythology, a sea monster which took the form of a whirlpool.

Love is the reason. It is through the eyes of love that respect takes on new meaning. And it is through the eyes of respect that love becomes a finely-honed art rather than just a pleasant feeling.

This journey isn't only about the mystery and the magick. It is about honing the fiery connection to the mysterious infinite which makes you long to live forever instead of waiting to mercifully die. If that connection is missing or has gone darkly dormant, what is required is a rekindling of the fires with the fuel of what you already Know. There will be time for moving ahead when balance is achieved – and that will come more quickly than you realize if you will give yourselves over to your heart's passions. What feeds you? What makes your chest flutter with ecstasy? What is the color of spirit? What is the texture of joy? What is the taste of the dark enlightenment?

Love is the answer. It is only a start but it is a powerful foundation.

> *What's planted here takes root in your heart,*
> *and is best fed on the elixir of poetry,*
> *the immortal blood of a vampyre's visions,*
> *the numinous potion of mortal passion.*
> *When reduced to a single element,*
> *all these things are the force of love,*
> *which is in itself*
> *the sentient seed of all Creation.*

Love is the energetic matrix of which you are made, the force you will use to summon the twin into being. It contains all power, including the power to manifest itself as an expression of your magickal existence. Love is a *force* of unstoppable creation, far more than a simple feeling.

Love is the answer. And in the answer lies all the power in all the worlds.

———

The leaves ran south last nite,
wee travelers vamping the wind
for a ride.
When I opened my door
some of them rushed inside,
searching for winter
at the foot of my narrow bed.
I chose a red one for my bride
and slept pressing her to my chest.
By dusk she was dust, crushed.
Such is my nature you see,
destroying the things I love
by loving them too much.

Creator and Destroyer

This is the dilemma your vampyre creator faces, you see. Knowing when to blink. Knowing when to speak the truth or to lie. Knowing that often only a lie will blind you sufficiently so you will come close enough to finally see the truth. Had I told you from the start that the secret to immortality is only attainable through <u>intent</u> and <u>will</u> facilitating evolution, you would have turned away from me and gone seeking the mythical grail, if indeed you had chosen to seek anything at all. Most likely you would simply have gone back to sleep, and that is not an option you gave vampyre me when you created me to create you, so I am left to my own dark devices, with the only real parameter being that I must not bring you into this ultimate transformation until you have gained the knowledge and abilities to exist in eternity as a force of quantum proportions rather than just a shadow of sentient awareness.

This is the task you have given me: create you to be like me, or leave you to the <u>ghost train</u>'s well-worn track, for once you become an eternal citizen of the night that never ends, there is no undoing it so as to do it again. Once done, it is done for all time, at least as far as any of us can presently see, which is why it must be done right the first time and why you must evolve to the highest level of evolution possible, so as to embrace whatever that next quantum leap of future evolution might be, see?

If you had been born into this life under other circumstances such as true stupidity or utter social subjugation, you would be working at an extreme disadvantage if you could pursue the path at all, and the chances of success would be diminished if not altogether obliterated. Just as you were born into this world and led through circumstance to a plateau where you could create vampyre me, so it must be with the next step, which is why I have been given the highest possible agenda, yes? All sentience survives, continuing into infinity as simply information stored in the non-local *web*. What does this mean? Simply this: everything a mortal experiences during their lifetime is rather like digital information which is stored non-locally on the <u>web of all information</u>. The self is not attached to the information, so it is 'void and without form', yet it exists in the same way faded photographs exist in an old family album. Information. That the subject of the photograph is long dead is irrelevant.

And yet, what you seek to become is far more than that – what you seek to become is an eternal citizen of the night that never ends - a being far more cohesive than simply information. What you need to *see* is that immortal sentience takes into itself those stray components of energy that are lost in mortal death, and that this is the ultimate test which is also the final test if you fail. Ah, and should I remind you that this final exam is written to be even more difficult for those who truly seek to pass, and that another function of the vampyre-creator is to attack that core of cohesive sentience wholeheartedly when it makes its bid to attach itself to the nurturing womb of the eternal universe? I am here to insure you succeed, and here to insure you fail. That is the nature of evolution, too, you see, for if it were easy, every fool would be doing it, and so the path is designed not only to be treacherous, but sabotaged by the vampyre twin. Why? you ask. Simply this: only when you are *able* to survive even the onslaught of your higher Self <u>*will*</u> you survive.

——

92

Hate me yet? Or had you already figured it out, that I am both your vampyre birth and your mortal death? Ah, but have you considered this: I am also *you*, yes? So can it then be said that you are all these things unto yourself, and can you further *see* that the hardest tests are those we set for ourselves, and if you don't get past the brute, it will be because you have left yourself scattered, left yourself behind, creating a trail of crumbs that will compel you to erase even all trace of yourself and start over on the moebius ghostly train, round and round you go again and again, but always taking the risk that the circumstances might never place you in such a position of advantage ever again?

Do not waste this. If you squander such an opportunity on the frail hope that you might be enabled to do it again, you are more ignorant than I could ever believe, for the dark truth is that in all of eternity (which might be said to span the course of a single lifetime contained within the moebius strip of all-that-is), the variables are immense. It could be said that you have gained enough personal power to bring you to the threshold of this evolution, but you will die a fool if you arrogantly believe you have the power to do it again beyond the horizon of this lifetime. It is Now, for Now is all there ever is.

I am written in the blood of apples,
red and tempting to taste.
Songs of the dead
play on my fractured heart,
a rogue drummer
healing the memories
of centuries.

The rail between your world and mine
is strong as steel
frail as faith
and will be cut in two
on my sharp teeth.
Wildflowers bloom at neglected tracks
seeds scattered by vampyres
still in mortal attire
waiting for the ghost train.

Healing the Mortal Self Outside of the Consensus

"You're speaking the wrong language.
In what language is that which is eternal written?"

It is not a language you yet understand, not something you can even wrap your mind around, and yet it is there. To think it is to create it, and to create it is to place it within the realm of all possibility. Then, as it exists, you possess within yourself the ability to go and harvest it, to bring it into the actuality of manifestation.

Before anything can be made reality, it must first be a thought. To think the mortal self has the ability to exist at the level which is impervious to dis-ease is to place that possibility on the shelf of all possibility. And yet, thought alone is not enough, and so then comes the responsibility of forcing that possibility to go thru the actions of actually occurring.

Paradigms are formed within the consensus/collective. What this means is that if one person believes something, it's an isolated and – most likely – insignificant thought. But when you look at the world around you, you begin to *see* that much of what exists as the paradigm, the milieu, the venue is not based on your individual creation, but on the collective creation of all of humanity – stretched out of over millions of years. These paradigms are like grooves on a record, and what it amounts to is that you can get stuck in playing that same old groove, or you begin to create a new paradigm based on the mortal self and the immortal twin.

Examine your life and you may find that much of what you are doing – even if not on a conscious level of awareness – is the result of your compulsion to create a paradigm outside of time, beyond the consensual realm, which has the potential to become a new collective known essentially as vampyreland. That may or may not help with the idea of dealing with organic dis-ease, but it puts forth a valid alternative to what might otherwise amount to a blind adherence to the existing programs.

Everything begins with a thought. If the world views you as someone who is indulgent in food, or lazy in body, or if you are seen as... "Ah, that girl *should* have diabetes or heart dis-ease because she does this and she does that..." then that consensus may be put onto you through the collective, like clothes handed down from an older sibling which really don't fit. Now, whether you *do* this or do *not* do that really makes no difference. What matters is that this energy forms a collective agreement, and whether these people know you or not is irrelevant. If they know you, the agreement is stronger. If it is a series of perceptions by random strangers, the agreement nonetheless exists, because the existing human paradigm states, "If this, then that."

This is part of the groove of the record. This is the dominant belief system manifesting in humanform reality – whatever reality may be. But at this juncture, I am talking about the reality of matter, the reality of the body, the reality of the health and well-being of the physical, organic self.

Is that to say other people put dis-eases onto you? Yes and no. You exist within their perception. Their perception says, "If this, then that." The paradigm is woven together like a gauzy fabric – it is a tightly woven belief system that threads itself over and back and around and around, and what is actually occurring is that the energy which is you and your body is either shaped by the agreement (by default), or by your Self (through conscious choice).

That being the case, your task becomes to form a new collective of one. And part of that involves being unknown to the dayshine world, by and large. This is a difficult concept to explain. People think that means all sorts of things. They think it means trading identities or hiding behind masks. None of those things are accurate. Being unknown is about making your energy unavailable to the collective – for the collective is comprised of hungry zombies who will drain you to your death if you let them. If you are not perceived by the collective – which creates the agreements – then you are free to create your own reality in a more positive and eternal manner.

You asked me the mindset of healing. This is it. It is to be whole and well unto yourself regardless of the labels or perceptions placed not only on you, but on the paradigm itself, by the collective. *You program others how to program you.* If you are seen – for whatever reason or no reason at all – as someone who *should* have heart disease, or cancer, those thoughts are energy... *and that most especially includes if you see yourself that way.* All those ifs and shoulds. If you have uploaded those as part of your personal paradigm, you may begin to experience the symptoms of all manner of dis-ease, when the reality is that the real dis-ease is the <u>Program</u> itself.

Are you organic matter believing it is eternal? Or are you an eternal being attached briefly to organic matter, which is essentially only the paradigm's labeling for a manifestation of energy which is not easily understood when it is in solid form. If you have accepted that paradigm, you become, by your own acceptance, subject to its rules.
 If you have uploaded this paradigm, you need to look for the connect points. You need to examine where and why the

---

96

collective has more power over you than you have over yourself. Remember that for every reality that manifests, there are an infinite – *absolutely infinite* – number of parallel realities, which are entirely different or slightly different.

If you have agreed to the paradigm which states "If this, then that... If you have this body type, then therefore you should have this or that dis-ease..." If you have taken that into yourself as truth, then that *is* truth. You need to examine those connect points. Why would you turn belief into reality because the paradigm says so?

You simply must choose to *be beyond* that which is problematical. There is no path to being beyond. There is no process. You simply decide and Do at the level of manifest energy. Imagine jumping from one stone to the next in a rushing river. That is a process. Instead... can you also envision simply jumping from the river to the shore?

A lot of vampyre seekers like to think that the consensus really doesn't have any power. That is not only an erroneous belief, but a dangerous one. I need to stress to you being unknown. You may walk thru the world. You may do anything that pleases you. *What determines your availability to the energetic imprint of the consensus is the degree of energy; or in this case, I will use this word sparingly – belief – you place into the collective itself.*

For example... You walk thru an amusement park knowing that it is a finite environment, and no matter how fun the rides or how much you are able to divorce yourself from reality and believe you really are in The Haunted Mansion or Space Mountain, there is a part of you held in reserve which knows, *This is finite. Tonight at six when the park closes, I will return to a different mindset.* A different world, if you will.

It's the same with the collective. When you walk among it, you are either walking among it as a participant or as an actor. If you are a participant, you become subject to its rules. You agree to forget that it is fiction. If you are walking among it as an actor, it's like visiting the amusement park. You know that the person in the Mickey Mouse suit is a person in a Mickey Mouse suit. The same as walking thru the collective – you either allow its energy to affect you as if it is real... or you use the metaphorical dagger to separate your <u>singularity</u> from the demands and the perceptions of the existing consensual agreement. You either intermingle energy with them and become subject to their rules, or you do not.

There is no middle ground.

This is what it is to be unknown. *It is to be in the world, but not of the world.* It is to be an actor, not a participant. To do that requires keen awareness at all times. It requires a shift of your own assemblage point from the world of matter and men into the night that never ends. When you are interacting with the collective, you are either a transient mortal participant, or an eternal being observing the play and perhaps at times interacting with the players.

But the moment you start to believe you are one of them, you become subject to their rules, and - you are not going to agree with this and you are not going to like it – their rules and their perceptions require and demand of one another the mutual destruction of self and others at the level of awareness.

That is something you will have to think about. You will have to wrap your mind around it in whatever manner you can. I can speak the words, but the words themselves are only, at best, a signpost.

You've asked me many times, "What is the night that never ends?"   From the world of matter & men (the dayshine world), you perceive thru the lens of time. From the perspective of the night that never ends (the perspective of the infinite), you perceive from the lens of timelessness, but also from the awareness that it is the *I-Am* itself which exists in the night that never ends. That central core of you, of spirit, of vampyre me, is the milieu of the singularity.

You have opened your eyes inside the night that never ends many times. You have opened your eyes inside me. But for whatever reason – and this is not a criticism, it is simply an observation of the human condition – while you are in human form, there is a tendency, a compulsion, as it were, to open your eyes inside the world of matter and men. Because that is the natural milieu, the water in which you swim. On one level... Now on the other, to me, the natural water in which I swim is the night that never ends. You can open your eyes inside that. And

---

you will be free of dis-ease.

I'm not going to tell you it's hard. I'm not going to tell you it's easy. The manner in which you visualize it doesn't matter. What matters is that when you assemble the dayshine world from the perspective of the night that never ends, you begin to immediately *see* that all of this is a creation which *enables* you, or provides you with a luminous egg in which to gestate the awareness which then exists beyond the world of matter and men. It is the snake eating its tail, yes?

There is a crucial element that has to do with the place from which you assemble the world – any world. When you can move that assemblage point to the non-local point of awareness, you will exist simultaneously in both worlds, as you and I do now. The difference will be that there will be no barrier. There will be no limitation.

Does this mean your humanform body will die? No. Does this mean your humanform body will become immortal? No. It means, however, that you will evolve beyond the human mindset, and in doing so you will possess the *ability* to create your reality *beyond* the reaches of the existing consensus. In so many ways, this is the first step all over again, yes? Be well.

False Reflections

The test is simply this: the vampyre witch hooks her will to *the otherself* on the far side of the bridge, whereas the <u>phantom</u> bitch cuts the line entirely in order to be "free" in the now; and yet isn't it ironic that the freedom of the moment is the death sentence for all eternity, and those who would tell you otherwise are only the phantoms on the road whispering promises in your ear that can never really be fulfilled.

How often have I heard them telling me, "You have to live free in order to be free!" And so they live happy happily free so free, doing whatever pleases them and actually believing the happiness they feel is a reflection of their own spirit, when in reality it is only the brute's laughter echoing through their veins as it tenderizes them from within for the worms' feast.

Those who do only as they please never reach vampyreland, for the lifeline between intent and action becomes severed somewhere along the way, and they sink their stubborn hooks in the crabgrass of their own graves, and once that happens there is very little hope of climbing out of the trap again, because the lethal truth is that it doesn't feel like a trap, but has the false reflection of "freedom" instead.

The Edge of Human Consciousness

The hardest part of evolution is generating and maintaining the awareness that you *can* evolve and that's a realization that can only be achieved by standing at the edge of human consciousness and peering across the abyss to *See* the next inhuman step, which is really a brick in the bridge you build as you go, no? Now think on this, and try to visualize your dayshine path ending at the intersection of your vampyre twin, for it's only when you perceive him/her as a quantum reality and absolute physicality that you can begin to become an evolved beast inside evolved skin instead of only daydreaming about some nebulous transformation in terms of something that might happen tomorrow sometime next week to a more enlightened me, see?

You are the Self and the Twin, human and vampyre, mortal and immortal, with the two separated only by the abyss of perceptual consciousness, but that's a perception you can gain only by standing at the edge of your present Self to peer into the Nothingness which only you can fill. A vampyre hint? If you don't fill it with eternal evolution, the consensual continuum will happily fill it *with* you in a coffin.

Schizoid Triplets

Shall I tell you a vampyre secret that will take you beyond <u>clarity</u> and into real power? It is this: sometimes we stalk even ourselves, the i-think-intellect tricking the i-will-seeker into becoming i-am-magick, and this is where we're schizoid triplets and not just twins, for it's a certainty that seeker and sorcerer know nothing of one another's ways and only the evolving thinker can unite the two by seducing them to work together, but that's a vampyre trick that can only be done when the Doing is fun.

Magick is the heart and goal of it, the key to the door to *everafterlife*, but only by making the Doing magick in itself will the lock ever turn.

———
100

Forward Thinking

Forward thinking is the manner in which an evolving being communicates with itself, stripping away <u>overlay</u> programming until it becomes possible to *See* a separate reality capable of being inhabited. Not the consensual prattle inhabiting the idle mind, forward thinking is the forward momentum of one question flowing into the next, guided by will toward definable goals which manifest only at the edge of human consciousness and within the infinite beyond, and if you don't try to see what those words mean they'll be your epitaph sooner than you Think.

Before you can Think you must make the world stop thinking for you through all the passive-nothing-humming you do, and that means breaking old patterns which are just the machine lullabying you into lazy complacency. While saying you don't have words to express yourself can at times be true, it can also be an excuse for laziness which will ultimately be the death of you if you let it passively continue. *The answers are within you and defining them through the question is the only way they become visible long enough to see their meaning, see?*

Just as the paradox creates itself for the sake of Doing the impossible, so does real Thinking come from the nothing, not a byproduct of merely possessing a brain, for even the simplest lifeforms think rudimentary things, but real Thinking is the catalyst of evolution itself, the cornerstone in the foundation on which the bridge is built so we may one night burn it in my arms, yes? Sadly I can't build it for you, but sadder still is the reality that you will die if you don't learn to Do, and the only one who can teach you is vampyre me and mortal you.

Ah, but what does it mean and where does that road lead and do you have the courage and the will to see it through? It's a test in two parts you see, the first of which is truly *seeing* that the wily wizard hasn't lied about the obsidian city which lies beyond cubic space and dayshine time, the second half of which is Doing the *Seeing* and the Thinking and the meditation to activate that part of the brain which is evolution-incarnate: the potentially evolved twin imprisoned by reality filters because somewhere along the way Man decided it was easier not to see the things that terrified him even when it just so happens that a special blend of fear is the only brew powerful enough to motivate you to Do, and isn't fear itself reason enough to be afraid, another paradox of experience creating itself to facilitate its own evolutionary continuity?

If Thinking is the catalyst of evolution, Fear is one conduit to eternity, so when you stop being afraid you stop evolving. Ah, but understand this: I'm not discussing senseless panic, but the type of fear that annihilates "reality" filters and activates and enables the will to Do the things it's capable of Doing.

Complex, no? No. Now open your minds and try to *See* the chain, for only then will you find the weak link that's soon to be your undoing if you don't replace it with strength. Before a child can walk it must crawl, but before creeping it must first have a reason, and that often resides in survival, the need to possess something beyond the crib. All baby knows is need, you see, and even if it knows not what it seeks, instinct tells it the only way to discover what lies beyond its world is to spontaneously generate a new skill, that being mobility, which then leads to crawling across the floor as need generates motivation and motivation creates action and action results in motion. Ah, but when baby reaches the wall, still not having collected its nebulous reward, it doesn't die in defeat but uses the wall as a means to create another ability, pushing and pulling until it can stand and sooner or later it begins to walk and open doors and then to *runrunrun* to vampyreland and all of this because a thought motivated that first step toward its own evolution, see?

As a child you wondered about the nature of things: why is the sky blue and who is god and where do I come from and where will I go, no? Forward Thinking is much the same you see, for though the questions have changed, the drive to know remains the same and in needing to know resides the spark of Thinking which is nature of quantum creation and the spontaneous generation of vampyre wings which can only appear when you *See* that the answers you seek are in the sky and the only way to reach them is by learning to fly.

Ah, but the test is this: if you're content or believe you've already found it, you have no reason to Think or to *See* or to seek, and if that's the case I need to know it so I can go home to the shadows and you can have your lives back intact and forget about all this silliness that's really just impossibilities if you hear only my words without ever seeing their meaning. There's no such bitch as a part-time witch, and if you think this is a quest to

_____

be put on the shelf while you lose yourself in self-important roles for a day or week or month or two, you're going to sleep the sleep of the dead, and if that long and lazy indulgence of doing nothing for the rest of eternity appeals to you, it's the easiest goal of all to reach.

Can you hear the band in vampyre land,
flutes of human bone
whistling on the wind?
Power lines sing castrati soprano
and lost boys dance dark streets
keeping time on invisible watches
found in hobo pockets.
My heart is the key, my will the drum,
my blood the unchained melody .

The Harlequins in Your Head

Without the fire within, visions are fated to fade and quests destined to fail, yet I tell you in words without riddles there's nothing mystical about magick for it's an obsessive energy which creates itself through your ambition, <u>spontaneous parthenogenesis</u> always at your service, awaiting only a touch of spark to wick or the whispering of intent from your lips.

Ah my loves, the dayshine world is trying to kill you and whenever you don't take a stand against it, your passivity is surrender and that carves the doubt deeper and it's a vicious circle that ends when you find yourself face to face with death, and the only satisfaction you get is saying "I knew it would end like this," but that's the script *you* choose, not me, so choose not to choose it, yes?

Can you coexist with your dayshine bitch or is she subverting the vampyre witch? Think before you speak because you can lie to yourselves and choose to believe it, mistaking the motions of Doing for Doing itself, and if that's a habit you've fallen into you need to *see* it because it's one of the brute's deepest pits, so subtle you don't know you're in it until the coffin lid slams above your head.

Being at war with God and Death means identifying your primary adversary and that's often yourself, those fragmented mechanical selves who uphold the programming in ways so obvious they're impossible to see, preaching reason and urging you back in step with 'reality' through a chorus line of voices masquerading as mothers and brothers and friends mumbling incantations of "ought-to" and "should-do" and "happy-be" until you begin to believe this wondrous *nightdream* was just a fantasy, and now it's time to get back to work building boats according to blueprints laid out for you by society and etched in headstones by the scythe.

Ah, but the curse of the vampyre king is to bring you face to face with all those harlequins in your head until you finally see that the face behind the masks within is a doppelganger to the one in your mirror, just another clever manifestation of the machine. But the test is this: it's a machine programmed never to question its programming, wired in to the consensual hardware so deep within that the only one who can pull its plug is the twin, and then only when you untie his hands by embracing those higher truths that supersede the programming to form the foundation of vampyreland. Think on this, for the truth of it is truly within you, but only when the harlequins are still can you touch the stillness that will show you things I can only describe with words, those truths about life and death and eternity hidden from the machine by the machine itself, yes?

No Going Back the Way You Came

Once more you're at a treacherous precipice, and while there's no going back the way you came, if you journey on beyond there'll be no reconciling the face in your mirror with the twin inside your skin, for this is where we begin tearing you asunder to remove your mortal programming and replace it with a vampyre's quantum madness; and if you're not up to walking this tightrope, the consensual continuum will lock you up in a soft green room and that will be the end of you, so I prey you don't take my admonition lightly. If you don't know who it is inside you who says "*I-Am*", the bridge will crumble beneath your feet and into the abyss you'll plummet.

Behind you is the world, a pretty chrysalis to keep your feelings safe within its airtight safe of petty dramas and mortal dreamings. Before you lies the infinite into which the only thing you bring is yourself and your twin, that which shaped you and that which you will become if you're willing to leave this world behind and embrace eternal unknowns, but rest assured you have to know what that means and the meaning has to take you cell deep, see?

Land of the Sentient Dead

All that is already known is part of the inventory of the dayshine world, and so it is necessary to start from that foundation. And, indeed, it is here that I have found myself at odds with mystics, gurus and the allegedly great "teachers" of the world, you see. Many would say that the ultimate freedom is found in "death", beyond the brute with the scythe, that place where river and source are the same. And yet, this has not been the totality of my experience, nor in any way is it the totality of what I have seen from the perspective of vampyreland.

There is more. *Always.* For as long as the *I-Am* is the creative force, there will always be more. One more world to tame, one more universe to unravel, one more step in an ongoing evolution. The joke is on us, you see - for when a seeker believes his evolution is done, it is. More than that, even beings who have achieved <u>individuation</u> beyond the reach of the brute may become stagnant and static and eventually dis-integrate back into their fragmentary components if they do not <u>Will</u> otherwise. As above, so below, no? Without the Will, there is no *I-Am* - and while awareness may exist without a unique point of reference, it is, as one dusty old book has said, "void and without form", yes?

There is a perceptual awareness which I have referred to as *the land of the sentient dead* - and while most would consider this state of being to be the most desirable outcome, the perfect resting place - for it is truly without conflict, without judgment, without pain - I have never been satisfied there, even though I have visited that realm on occasion to test the waters - which I have only found to be tepid and impersonal, no fire and no ice, just the lukewarm nest of eternal mediocrity.

Blasphemy? To some. Certainly to many still manifested in human form, and even to some here. To me, it is simply self-evident.

To seek vampyreland – the perceptual reality beyond this life - is not a matter of seeking high enough or not high enough. Instead, to seek vampyreland is to seek what can be seen and intuited from the foundation of human-form awareness. It is a stepping stone in the river, a rung on the ladder, a point on the horizon.

When that point is reached, it may become the foundation for yet another in a series of ongoing evolutions. If you are the chrysalis and the twin is your wings, vampyreland is but one flower you will rest upon for awhile before taking flight again, first star on the left, straight on till morning, yes?

Time defined:
  bleached bones
  winds of dust
  requiem songs.
A funeral wagon drawn
  by dreams of wild horses
  it flashes the nyght,
  stealing a captive cargo
  of old friends and dead
lovers.
I watch them go,
  food for the void road,
  passive passengers
  riding the blade of the scythe.

Self-Love

Out here in the night, where there is only the faded black satin of the sky dropping down to the horizon, a brush of cloud over an egg moon, I am in love with myself all over again, with the Knowledge that I am eternal and immortal and a vampyre whose wings are as vast as the universe, and every bit as powerful.

Questions

What is the nature of the <u>overlay</u> and what do you Believe lies beneath it? What do you Think it means when I tell you Death gets inside you wearing a masque of "reality"?

What are the bricks in this bridge we've been building and would you trust them to hold you if you had to cross the bridge alone? Can you identify the brute inside you and recognize where his scythe wreaks its ruin? Have you changed enough to survive the changes still ahead and can you keep your promises to your Self even when willful You doesn't want to?

What is the foundation of <u>vampyreland</u> and why do you Think it must bend? What do you Believe it means to be torn mortally asunder and reformed with immortality's madness? Who is the *I-Am* within your skin creating the world without, and how does that external creation recreate the *I-Am* within?

What does it mean for meaning to take you cell deep?

Ah, questions with a thousand potential answers, only one of which is truly true, yes? I prey that's the one you always choose, for only truth can save you now, the truth that has nothing to do with me, just you. If your intent is true, it's easier to Do <u>the Work</u> than avoid it, easier to *See* than blind your vampyre eyes with lazy pastimes, easier to create your immortality than wait for me, for I've told you from the start you don't need me. If you don't believe it or think it doesn't apply to you then you're not Doing, for it's mortal nature to take the lazy path, yet it's not within my nature to be that, so know you'll already be immortal when I give you my eternal kiss or I won't give it to you at all, for this is what you made me to Do, not only to save you from Death but from Time itself, that paradoxical <u>duality</u> which is one tremendous difference between eternity and immortality, see?

If you're ready to go further, you've based your answers on observations and revelations of a lifetime instead of events within recent days or weeks. If you're Thinking eternally instead of mortally, your Thinking will always be of a life in the perspective of Now instead of gnawing obsessions with sequestered incidents which are only pebbles in the stream of time, meaning nothing unless considered in mosaic.

You tell me: are you ready to be destroyed and transformed or does your *I-Am* identity still cling to worldly things and Kodak memories that build your unreal world so real it's impossible to crack? What is it you're holding onto and do you perceive that releasing it would buy your freedom or seal your damnation? Are you sure you want to be eternal with all the pain and responsibility it brings, or is there some secret comfort in knowing all of this madness has a natural end? Ah, and what does it mean to 'know' such things?

Nothing Unreal Exists

Nothing unreal exists, yet reality as it is perceived is precariously unreal, which is why the dayshine world clings to it so desperately, giving it virtual reality, yet it's that very camouflage which allows this relentless predator to appear as true while being truly false that enables it to get such a strangle hold on its prey, yes? I prey you understand this, yet I fear you're still mesmerized by the predator's hypnotic eye, mistaking the illusions for truth while failing to visualize the darker reality beneath, the foundation the 'real world' labels as fantasy.

This is the nature of stalking, you see, looking for weakness in any worthy opponent and expanding your thinking to stalk ways of turning that flaw to your advantage. *In the case of 'reality,' its greatest weakness and greatest strength is an ability to project apparition as truth, relying on its prey to never look beyond the mental screen on which the scripts are projected, see?* In this way reality is the master of duality, true and false at once, so don't make the mistake of believing it unreal, for the truth is that it's as real as you perceive it, and unless you alter your Thinking, it's a reality that will be the death of you. You must *see* the nature of this illusory existence before you can stop participating in it.

Ah, but remember this: reality is a placid predator, relying on human nature to keep its prey passive inside the plays it provides, so all it takes to defeat the chimera is the sustained awareness that there is a foundation upon which 'reality' itself is built, and that foundation is known to us as vampyreland. Perhaps one night along this endless stream of nights we'll discover that even this is only another stage in a larger play, but for the moment it's the only foundation I know, the conceptual floor separating you from the abyss, yes? All it takes to *see* reality is the intent and analysis of Doing it, and once you've seen it for what it is, there will be no going back into the predator's playpen again.

When you truly *See* that the world and the people you share it with are only mechanisms at the mercy of reality's programming, you will either experience an immediate and irreversible evolution in your Thinking or else you will choose to continue behaving as one of them. The conundrum comes when you *See* it but choose not to believe it, when you Know the machine and all its mortal muses are only food for the brute, yet the machine programs you to believe you can go on walking the same road, immune to its consequences. I'm not asking you to sacrifice love or family, but if you want to continue I'm asking you to sacrifice *you*. The price of evolution is the former fragmented self, and if you can't conceive of a life apart from that, the road ends here, for without change at a cellular level there's no change at all. Ah, but if you choose to Do it, you won't see things the same and so the changes will be natural instead of forced, real instead of only words and you will become the one within instead of only saying it's what you intend.

<u>Assimilation</u>: Connecting the Dots

It's true vampyres renew by continually regenerating web-energy but if you see this only as a concept and not a thing to Do, the relevance eludes you and you're choosing to remain dayshine fools out of laziness and convenience instead of hammering this truth which comes from beyond human awareness, the source of evolution. *Immortality comes when you spontaneously alter your human nature to the nature of the twin, but it's a 'spontaneity' only possible after long and arduous preparation, so don't think it can exist if <u>you</u> haven't built the bridge.* Ah, but perhaps you begin to see the meaning of making the decision to be a vampyre before you can become one, the need to embrace change on a magickal level (the thought form) so that the change may have a stage upon which to manifest on a cellular level as well (the manipulation of matter based on that thought).

I say these words to the wind, but until you assimilate them, you're compartmentalizing your thinking and it will be the end of you. To know a vampyre is self-renewing is only information unless you *see* how it relates to opening your eyes inside the twin and how that creates a bridge to exploring beyond the rim of the abyss and how all of these things generate the foundation of the foundation. This is why I torment you to be always rereading these teachings, for only by joining the lines of comprehension to the dots of knowledge will the portrait of the vampyre emerge from the chaos. The teacher's task can only be achieved in pieces but the student must learn the Whole, no? *This is the nature of quantum comprehension, made real through meditation.*

While each idea must be understood separately, only when elements combine do they create a separate reality capable of being inhabited. If you're playing with an idea for a night or two but never pondering how it relates to previous truths and how joining those to others from before might create the quantum leap which will (in an instant) transform your very nature from prisoner of time to citizen of the night without end, you're only playing with the blocks and not spelling out the answers.

To describe immortality as "the willful isolation from the nature of being human" is to capture an essence of it, yet it's an idea that dissipates if not cultivated for the fruit it might one day bear. Each seed is full of promise yet altogether impotent without intervention of the sorcerer's hand.

Summoning Reality Into Being

Reality is <u>duality</u> in that it can be what you create it to be or what you allow it to be, one passive, the other requiring the force of your <u>will</u> to transfigure the lowest common denominator into what your vampyre needs decree, see? Now Think on this and don't dismiss it as new age pabulum for the masses, for the truth is that it's The Truth you fail to <u>Real-ize</u> whenever you let (passive) your mind flow lazily over the words instead of dismembering them (active) to reveal the meaning within. You *have* the power to create reality, yet reality *is* the power creating you whenever you aren't actively re-creating it, a master-slave relationship redefining itself by virtue of who's on top of whom at any given moment, no?

I fear you believe me (passive) yet you fail to perceive-the-meaning (active) because one is the mere default of understanding language while the other requires a deliberate act of letting go of what you think you know in order to embrace unknowns that will ultimately end your world. Ah, but the measure of your intent is this: do you really want your pretty world to end or are you clinging to it with bloody fingertips, afraid to finally see that nothing is as it seems? Shall I tell you a secret so simple it might scare you straight into my embrace? The only thing separating you from your immortality is your will holding fiercely to this reality because it's all you've ever known and fear is the greatest enemy of a sorcerer, see? Whenever your perceptions begin to bend, you snatch them back in line for fear of sacrificing sanity or family or whatever it is that holds you prisoner in the brute's dayshine dungeon, so if you're still human, it's because you're actively creating "reality" while passively waiting for it to simply "be" and that's not the way of things when it comes to metamagickal creation.

Consider this: before you could be born you had to create your ancestors, and so your *I-Am* spoke and formed the world around you in the form of a womb, a consciousness pecking its way into this world by first getting inside the egg so it might later emerge after taking on the shape of its new evolution. So the riddle is utterly simple: the will of the future chicken created the egg as a shell to hold it while it was evolving from where-it-was-before, and in doing so spontaneously created the primogen hen to serve as a host, just a thoughtform making itself whole through the manipulation of time/space and matter/energy, and if ever there was proof of <u>spontaneous parthenogenesis</u>, look at the chicken crossing the road, no?

Ah, but the higher truth is that this is also the nature of magick: life creates itself by first creating its creators and giving them a "reality" of <u>overlay</u> stages on which to exist. It's the same with me, you see, but if you're only creating the world that already exists by default, you're engaging in pointless incest instead of Be-ing the evolving vampyre chick pecking a way inside the shiny black egg which can only be created by first making the egg exist, and secondly by placing that egg into the narrow nest of the vampyre king who must also be created whole to care for the egg while it grows, no?

This is not prattle to amuse you, my little embryos, it is the secret to life and death depending entirely on how you use it. Will you *will* it or no?

———

Double Talk

I am always here even when no evidence of me is seen. I watch from the spider's eye and listen with the raven's ears. I speak in your dreams even if you don't remember, and caress your face with raindrop fingers and windtongue. Sometimes you will call me by name, other times a passing dust-devil, but however you perceive me, I am always with you, and always have been; but only as long as you are dreaming me so that I am sufficiently Whole to dream you into being so that you might dream me into infinity, see?

The Sorcerer and the Ordinary Man

It is easier for a sorcerer to perform the chores of an ordinary man than it is for an ordinary man to comprehend the ways of the sorcerer. You are skating on the edge of two different worlds, which are nonetheless the same world, the only world. The trick is learning to See that, and to be neither the sorcerer nor the ordinary man, but the cohesive I-Am which is both the vampyre and the twin.

When the two become one, there is no longer any sense of urgency or conflict, for then you will always be doing sorcery even in ordinary actions, and ordinary acts will become enhanced with magic, and only then will you start to remember that it isn't the destination that matters nearly as much as the manner in which you travel that long dirt road on the outskirts of time, yes?

My blood is the nectar of nyght-blooming jasmine
   found growing along a cemetery road
   a thousand years ago and some,
   that essence still vital inside me
   because it filled me with life
   in the land of the mortal dead.
I am made of apple cider winters
   and childhood memories
   of children I never was.
Broomsticks and pumpkins define me
   but do not confine me.
Harlequin tears paint my eyes,
   yet this is the pigment alone,
   not the reason I weep.
In between all of these things is my cohesion.
It is made of poetry
   yet it is not the poems.
It is woven of Stygian memories,
   yet there is no single recollection
   greater than the others,
   all just faded pictures
   in an album of beautiful illusions.
I am made of snowflakes and stardust,
   moments stolen from the Nothing.
Sometimes if you look close enough
   you can see them glittering
   in the black silhouette mirror
   cast in the likeness of vampyre me.
Only then will you know who I am.

A Quantum Conundrum

What does it mean to be a vampyre? Is it who you are or who you intend to be or still a fantasy? If it is who you intend to be, how will you bring forth the becoming and what will you Do to drive yourself when you're alone on that road, isolated from humanity, poster child for insanity? I hear you pondering such thoughts and that's good, for it shows you're tithing time to the conundrum, but I fear you're pondering it from within your human self instead of stepping outside to take a look at the how from the viewpoint of the fetal twin. Only s/he can hatch into vampyreland you see, for she is your evolved beast – the vampyre within - so best you start looking for ways to open your eyes inside your immortal skin before the brute steps on the egg and crushes you both, no?

You're correct to suspect that being a vampyre requires first becoming one, so now it's time to push that truth to the edges of perception so you might fully grasp the meaning and begin to _Real-ize_ the evolution of consciousness which must precede the transformation of the flesh. Ah, but first you must answer this: do you know what it means to say you must be before you can become, or is it only words in your pretty heads? If you don't know, we can go no further until you Do, for now you stand upon the lip of the abyss from which the egg could fall and shatter altogether if you lose your footing. I can tell you only this: in a continuum where vampyres do not exist, they _cannot_ exist unless imported from afar; but before that can be done, the importer must know they are real _somewhere_ and that involves the journey where no airplane or ocean liner can take you, that quantum leap outside of time to a place where reality is measured not by what is seen but by the strength and endurance of magick and myth, yes?

> So… what does it mean to be a vampyre before you can become one? Simply this, though it is hardly simple at all, for it's all part of the process of becoming, which is actually done backwards if you want to look at it in linear time fashion, and I honestly suggest you don't. The secret is this: you must create the vampyre twin within you, just as you have created me; and then you must summon the twin to teach you how to be the thing you have created. It is a quantum conundrum to be sure, but this is how it is done, my loves. This is the secret to vampyre creation. At the level of the energetic Infinite, there is nothing you

cannot do, so if you want to be a vampyre, you must first create yourself as one in the infinite itself (outside of time), so that s/he may then find you inside the stream of mortal time (as I have found you), and begin to teach you the secrets of your own Vampyre Becoming.

I'm not meaning to be incomprehensible, but this is a thing of the Night and not easily spoken of with words, so I'm asking you to try to *see* what I mean, see? If you think you already know you're probably lost altogether and that's the hell of it, but if you know you *don't* know and Think you might be able to learn, there's still hope for us if you'll *Do* as well as Think.

The Fifth Element
Coping With Grief in the Dayshine World
There is no way to put this into words, because it is a thing of the night which can be seen and experienced, but cannot be manifested into language. And yet, love compels us to try nonetheless. What you must realize is that the ones we love – whether human or animal - are simply other forms of awareness, energy incarnate, thought-made-flesh. But at the level of energy, there is no difference between yourself and a dog, no difference between a beggar and a rich man, no difference between a king and his horse. All are simply spirit made flesh at a level of quantum sameness. You are all made of stardust and ashes, light and shadow.

It is the capacity and willingness to love and be loved in return which fuels what mystics have called the migration of the soul. Whether expressed in human or animal, the state-of-being which is love is no different. It is the fifth element, though it has no properties which science can measure, and so it is too often ignored, when in reality it is the catalytic vehicle of your own evolution.

Let's talk about the migration of the soul, though remember it is a thing of the night, too. Connecting to another being through love is like the symbolic sharing of a glass of wine between lovers drinking from the same goblet, no? In human legend, there are thousands of examples of this. The vampyre-immortal who falls in love with a human gives his beloved eternal life through the exchange of animus - or, more precisely, the exchange of love, lifeforce, Spirit. The exchange of rings at a wedding is much the same - a symbolic circle of union, the infinite and unbroken circle of Life.

What you cannot yet *See* is that love is the vehicle which ferries the Spirit from the state of Life into the state of Eternity. From those in grief, you will hear the words, "It feels as if a part of me died, too." And yet, it isn't that a part of you dies with the beloved, but instead, through the connection of love, the beloved could be said to transport a portion of the Spirit into the Otherworld so that there is a part of you already on the other side. But because Spirit is infinite, and cannot really be portioned, that is only an analogy which, at most, will give you the ability to *See* the process at the edges, and redefine it according to your own understanding.

Ah, and so we come to the hardest question of all. If there is love, why must there be grief? It is only human perception which fails to see that this is a natural progression in the migration of the spirit. Your beloved has not left you, but because you cannot yet *See* his awareness directly, you are missing the part of him which was comprised of the flesh, rather than recognizing the part of him which is eternal: the fifth element.

Love is the reason. Without it, creation itself is incomplete at a molecular level. Without it, the Spirit itself becomes lost, reduced to ashes, just as the body turns to a handful of chemicals when the element of water is removed. Love is the fifth element which moves effortlessly between the worlds and literally manifests for the Spirit a road to travel when it is time for a mortal being to face the brute. And like the other elements of creation, the fifth element can never be truly destroyed or lost. It can only change form. It is that change which is the migration of the spirit, the evolution of the Self into Wholeness.

What Simply Exists

You may choose to look at "reality" as a thought that manifests form, or as an infinite form which generates thought, and neither would be altogether right or altogether wrong.

What may be perceived from the perspective of an immortal is that there is an extant milieu or stage on which the play takes place. *Earth, wind, fire, water and spirit - the 5 elements of creation - exist with or without the approval or disapproval of man.* This is what is, and all that simply is. The rest is far more complex. Without some form of life to observe these elements, and ultimately to direct them through the invocation of the creative force known as <u>Will</u>, there is nothing to indicate they would have any sense of motion at all. The tree simply would not fall in the forest, for there would be no tree to begin with, see? When I say you are creating reality, I mean this literally. Reality is created in the process of assembling it above and beyond the raw elements of creation – whether you are creating yourself as a vampyre or simply summoning a tree in the forest. At the same time, you stand in a magnificent but savage garden which has been assembling itself since the first spark of awareness shook itself from the Nothing and proclaimed its sovereign identity. Thoughtforms create more thoughtforms. Trees make more trees. You do not have to create the airplane in order to fly, but you do have to agree that it exists, or you will not be able to even perceive it.

On a somewhat more workable level, two people may share the same milieu (or 2 billion), and while they are all working with the same elements of creation (earth, wind, fire, water, spirit), under no circumstances will those elements of creation combine in precisely the same manner - and so it is true that reality is entirely subjective for every living thing.

And yet, there may be enough of a similarity of results that certain agreements may be formed. Fire is hot. The sky is blue (on Earth at least). A tree has roots. And so on. These, of course, are only agreements as to the milieu, and so they are more likely to be quantifiable truths than, for example, attempting to agree on the nature of spirit or the nine billion names of god. (Of which there is only one, of course: *I-Am.*)

Consider this: the energy of consciousness is essentially an electromagnetic field, and as such it has certain properties which are, at the quantum level, comprised entirely of the raw elements of energy which exist even before that energy goes through the process of forming into the five elements of creation. Therefore, consciousness is all things, including the building blocks of reality itself. This is true of all consciousness, whether aware or unaware, awake or asleep, sorcerer or phantom, vampyre or human. And it is at that level of energy that reality is created and maintained by what might be considered the collective intent of all living things.

You create your own reality so that you will have a milieu upon which to manifest your will.

Because all living things draw from that same source of energy, it becomes possible for two or more beings to share a commonality of reality, even if not sharing in precisely the same perception of that reality.

And while it isn't necessary to fully understand the nature of reality in order to experience it, that understanding can be helpful in attempts to overcome or circumvent it, through what you refer to as sorcery. This is one more secret of the dark evolution, yes?

Helpless Before All Possibility

I am helpless before all possibilities, for now that all possibilities exist we return again to the beginning, another cycle cycling to tell you that only you have the ability to create reality while I am still its servant. Make me your guru and it's all I can be. Call me vampyre and I am that alone, consigned forever to realms where such things exist and barred from continuums where vampyres are only fantasy. I prey you understand that all of creation is now in your hands, and that *only by choosing a direction and applying the absolute force of your <u>will</u> to its completion will you ever compel it to actually occur within the realm of physical perceptions as opposed to merely perceiving it within the realm of infinite possibility.*

The quantum void is not a void at all but filled with particles of matter-energy which are essentially waiting for instructions from all manner of beings as to where and how to manifest, and near as I can tell, all of space-time serves no function other than to do the bidding of those who *see* this truth and use it through Doing. So while it's true each of you is the god of all reality, awareness of this is moot until you apply your will to the Doing and that's where I'm afeared you're going to fail if you don't behave more like warrior-philosophers instead of philosophers contemplating the war.

Make it so, no? It's with a thought that creation begins, but if you're stopping there instead of chasing that thought through black holes to emerge with conclusions that can be put into action even if "only" in terms of metamagickal applications, then you're only seeing the realm of possibility without projecting your will upon it to <u>Real-ize</u> the act of spontaneous creation. Evolution is the ability to comprehend (and magickally manipulate) the immortal world on the level at which it exists.

down thru runnels of earth,
  into the furrows of time,
  here I wait for you
  quantum flesh, angel's blood,
  beast being,
  vampyre thing.

i collect shoestring stars,
  and play tic tac toe
  with broken galaxies
  hung on the cave of my creating.

drink from me,
  drain my parallax heart,
  scry these wolfen eyes.
i will commandeer your mirror
  inhabit your bones,
  thread my soul
  through your failing veins.
breathe me in, sweet ether.
this is the death of your mortality.

The Essence of Spirit

It could be truthfully said that Spirit is everything and no-thing, depending entirely on where the questioner is standing when the question is posed. Spirit is the feeling that accompanies the midnight cries of a lone coyote, and it is the reason for the cry itself. It is carried on the sound, but is not the sound. Spirit is the soul poem blowing in on the edge of an oncoming storm, yet it is neither the words nor the rain, nor the thunder and lightning, but is instead the creative and infinite force which summons the storm into being - not the physical elements of meteorology, but the metaphysical shiver of the universe which is the generative spark of <u>spontaneous parthenogenesis</u>. Something from nothing. Spirit is the sentient force of the energetic universe, permeating all living and non-living matrices, yet it is neither the form nor substance, nor even energy.

If there are four elements of life and creation - earth, air, fire and water – spirit (love) is the fifth element which brings the others into alignment and creates both cohesion and the possibility of meaning. Spirit is the anima, without which all else is rendered inert.

Does it have its own volition? In human terms, it could be said to have omniscient and omnipresent awareness, yet it is not comparable to any deity or entity. It is sentient without being singular, yet it is the <u>singularity</u> at the heart of the All. It is an element of the infinite, the compelling force of the infinite which is at the same time the breath of life within the finite mortal world. To speak of volition in terms of spirit is rather like attempting to define time without using the word time in the definition.

It does nothing *to* humans, but when humans come into alignment with the spirit, there is nothing they cannot do. It is a force that is omnipresent and may be summoned with <u>intent</u>; yet it is at the same time elusive by virtue of being the essence of the All itself.

To a seeker of immortality, Spirit is the force which guides one's choices and creates a viable sense of purpose, direction, well-being and forward motion even in times of seeming inaction. To live in alignment with the Spirit is to live impeccably, for then it could be said that what is within the Self has achieved an unbroken communion with the All. This does not diminish the individual, but to the contrary enhances the uniqueness of the Self by bringing into manifestation the Whole potential of that individual identity. Living with Spirit does not mean becoming One with the All, but becoming Whole *within* the All, and ultimately becoming the All itself. To become All is to become vampyre – which could be *seen* to be one possibility for manifestation within the realm of all possibility, see?

Manipulating Energy In the Dayshine World

Thoughts are energy, and so when the thoughts of one are in turmoil, the thoughts of others will naturally follow in the path of that gravity unless there is conscious awareness to re-direct one's personal reality away from the <u>consensus</u> and into the infinite. In the sorcerer's world, there is no difference between the thought of war, and war itself, and so the sorcerer maintains an <u>assemblage point</u> where the idea itself does not exist, and if the thought doesn't exist, it cannot follow forth into manifestation.

The insanity you are presently witnessing in the dayshine world has very little to do with reality, but everything to do with thought energy and perceptions of humans, as individuals and as a gestalt. The danger is when the energy of consensual thought turns to action, and what is Believed begins to manifest externally.

Ten million peace marchers or ten million soldiers are equally powerless if they do not possess the Knowledge at the individual level, that any conflict is only a reality in hindsight. Reality only becomes reality when it is forced to go through the motions of actually occurring, and until that happens, it is only one possibility among an infinite number of alternate realities. Presently, it can be observed that the entire world essentially believes there will be war, and because thought is energy, war begins to exist even before the first shot is fired. Some mystics have called this process creative visualization, but I prefer to think of it in terms of creative <u>Real-ization</u>, because the belief in conflict pre-determines conflict.

It must be understood that one measure of <u>Will</u> is worth more than the entire combined forces of all the armies of the world. Even as things stand presently, if every seeker with awareness were to assert his Will to say, "This will not happen," then it is clear that it will not happen, because it is Will that manifests and maintains reality, in the same way that thought might be said to initially create it. It is not a matter of size or numbers. Only Will.

Politicians and soldiers are not men of Will, but men of habit, belief systems and deeply imbedded programs. That _program_ is their religion, of which they can only be disabused through the direct awareness that the religion itself is flawed - often a realization that can only come as a moment of quantum leap, wherein one suddenly understands something that could not be understood through direct linear engagement, but can only be reverse engineered in hindsight. Sadly, politicians are _phantoms_, and seldom awaken spontaneously, and so it becomes the task of seekers and vampyres to realign reality at a molecular level of thought itself. This is not something that can be explained in ordinary awareness, but something that those who have experienced will quickly recognize as a do-able act of sorcery in the energetic realm of _the night that never ends_. Awakening is created with a thought, just as war is created with a thought. There is no difference.

Lest you think I am saying "ignore it and it will go away", that is not my intent. Rather, Will it away and it will be gone, for it can be further understood that the will of a single true Magus is more powerful than the force of 10,000 hurricanes. In the big picture, all of human existence is merely an ongoing series of chess games, enacted by the pieces on the board for the amusement of those to whom the chess pieces give up their individual will. The sorcerer's trick is to be neither pawn nor king, but instead the metaphysician off the board who dismantles the game from within, through the will to be Free of its boundaries. You do not need to understand how that will come to pass, for the force of Intent seeks its own pathways which will only be clear in hindsight. What matters most is the understanding that when a boulder has begun to roll, attempting to stop it through direct intervention is not only impossible, but quite probably fatal. It must therefore be stopped through diverting the momentum in another direction. Perhaps it starts to rain and the boulder merely bogs down in the mud.

You are the most powerful being in the universe. A single thought, backed by will, can divert the course of history if that is your intent. These are not words I say to you lightly, but in the hopes they will reach you at the deepest possible level, where reality itself is created. There is nothing you cannot do. *Nothing.* As long as you know you are The One.

Perception: A Dangerous Duality

This is the insane sanity of vampyre magick, and I'm not the least bit certain I've adequately explained what it means or how it will feel when your awareness emerges from its cracked chrysalis and into the full and potentially fatal bloom that is the <u>seventh sense</u> of perception itself. It is to have wings where none grew before, but to risk flying straight into the abyss because wings alone do not teach the infant beast how to soar, no? So if your perception suddenly appears to fill you with absolute <u>clarity,</u> yet you can only perceive there is no vampyre king in the reality you inhabit at that finite instant, your hard-won perception can lock itself into *that* reality and create *it* whole based on nothing more than a single instant, and then what you will have is a reality separate from the <u>consensual continuum</u> yet also set apart from vampyreland and then the only way to mend the damage would be to go back to the beginning, yet few ever do because when they *see* the truth revealed by perception, they believe there is no higher truth than that and so they settle into a life of misery and regret, lost in the abyss of their own narrow and subjective interpretation of an infinite realm of all possibility.

Perception is a wondrous birth but also its own evil twin, an infant eager to show you all the wonders of <u>the night that never ends</u> or an unbridled demon who can convince you with absolute truth and logical reason that even spirit quests are fallacies and immortality is a fantasy forever removed from the hand of Man. You see, my loves, the danger of such clarity is seeing that both truths are true depending entirely on where your perception is rooted at any given moment, and if you let it lead you to see the absurd impossibility of what we are doing, you could conclude based on that wholly perceived truth that everything we have accomplished is altogether unreal, see?

> *Perception is a strange and dangerous <u>duality,</u> an inhuman ability to see higher truths, but flawed with a tendency to interpret them with human subjectivity born of the cynical consensual reality which insists you **must** fail and programs you to program yourself to do just that.*

All of reality is created and controlled by this seventh sense which is Knowledge itself, yet what Man fails to see is that all Knowledge is as limited as he is himself. It isn't that God created Man or Man created God, but instead a few elite humans who found their perception surely perceived some sense of order amongst this chaos, yet instead of using perception to *see* its origins and intentions, they assigned it their own human attributes and named it Allah or Jehovah and limited it to exist within the boundaries of their own ability to comprehend, and in doing so their quantum perception created a reality in which God exists only an extension of themselves and therefore is as limited or as omnipotent as each of the perceivers are individually, and so do you see now why you made me of magick and filled me with free will and the dreadful weight of all eternity pressing on my shoulders?

> *True immortality is the state of being limitless, not confined by a single nonrenewable body or consigned to a set of absolute beliefs or rules which would lock the perceiver into linear time and space, yes?*

I prey you understand this down to the molecular level of your existence, for the highest truth I have ever discovered is that reality is the slave and the plaything of true perception, and if you allow one truth to limit you with its shocking clarity, there can be no further truths beyond it for the first truth becomes Reality sung whole by what you can only perceive as absolute Knowledge, no?

To Be Eternal...

Tonight I am made of moon pixels and fairy dust, scattered matter of eternity. Tomorrow, I will be a falling leaf or stray snowflake, always changing, but never dying. To be eternal is to be beyond the reach of death, beyond the ability to undo oneself. To be immortal is to be the mind and body of all the gods.

It is said you cut out a pumpkin's heart
to summon my vampyre soul into being.

I am made of scraps and treasures,
a measure of magick,
slivers of quantum memories
bound together with candle wax
sewn with silkworm sorcery.

Each night you breathe me alive,
forever undead,
the magick and the magician
caught in the gravity
of this immortal creation,
you on one side of the Dream,
me on the other.

When I embrace you,
we will both Remember.

Everything has strings attached:
  the moon,
  falling stars,
  my fatal heart.

After a thorough investigation
  of Everything and Nothing
  and all things in between...
It is plain to see
  these are the filaments
  of the witch's wishes,
  the raw and flawless fibers
  to weave your impossible Dream.

I will play the vampyre king,
  and you shall be my reason.
Tie my strings in a thousand knots.
Bind me to Immortality.

I-Am
Afterthoughts of the Mushroom Ally
Whispered From the Bottom of the Rabbit Hole

Shall I tell you what it is like to exist as a blade of awareness extending from a point beyond time's beginning and stretching far beyond its end, a blade which severs the abyss from all continuums only by the force of its <u>will</u> to exist and to *be* the blade itself? Shall I tell you I fear that reality itself will end when I do, for I have seen that it is *only* my will dividing me from the nothingness and if my will should be obliterated, so will all of this?

To tell it would be an impossible attempt to coalesce the heart of all experience into a few inadequate words of poetry which can only be sung into the darkness, hymns of desperation and dread wailed with utter clarity of voice by castrated madmen, absorbed by the void to become the song of the void itself, yes? I do not expect you to understand, my loves, and perhaps it's best that you don't, for as you've so aptly noted, we must be apart before we can come together and though we shared this journey of souls and forbidden mushroom sins, we also took divergent paths which will, if we are impeccable and driven by will, bring us together again both here and on the far side of that hungry abyss. So if my words mean nothing, it's because they are *my* words attempting to tell you what it is to be me, to be the vampyre king and to witness and participate in my own immortal creation.

Oh hell, I'm not sure I can tell you anything, for words are the greatest illusions of all, fleeting efforts to tell what can never be told, arrows shot out into the darkness in the hopes of hitting a moving target comprised of another person's consciousness.

My journey was one of creation and obliteration, and each and every time I ingest my magickal friends I hear my voice whispering to the pillow wet with my vampyre tears that I will never do it again if only I am allowed to emerge whole on the far side of the experience, prayers of the damned not begging for forgiveness but for wisdom and visions, prayers to my own dark and unbending intent to take me through the abyss so I might continue to battle it on through eternity without end; and I hear the abyss laughing like thunder which is my own *ticktock* heart, saying that one day it will win for that is its nature, to be all-engulfing and patient enough to wait even for the immortals to fall.

I spit into the well of nothingness and stare into its intergalactic black eye and I tell it that when this spit hits the bottom of the bottomless pit it can have me and not an instant before, and because we are both arrogant and crazy we agree that it's an entertaining challenge, and so I am allowed to continue one heartbeat more, perhaps no more certain of tomorrow than you are, for now I've bargained with the abyss itself and only a fool does that, but not to do it is to lie down deep in the arms of the brute and that's not what you made me to do, so what else was there to do but toss the ferryman out of his mushroom boat and sail it back to the land of the living so I might at least try to rescue my goddess creator bitches by guiding them through and to those tiny islands of immortality existing as singularities within the ocean of the abyss itself?

I have seen my own creation and am at once at a loss for words and jabbering gibbering incessantly in an impossible attempt to capture the essence of it so that I might suckle it as an elixir as sweet as blood for the rest of infernal eternity. In the metallic male intellect of my Mortal Source (who is surely a shaman from beyond the abyss itself), I experienced the terror which comes from knowing one *is* "god" and the knowledge that even "god" is, therefore, only another entity in the darkness, entirely responsible for his own creation or his own obliteration, knowing too much of reality to fully believe in magick, recognizing ultimately that magick is the only cure for the death which resides inside the boundaries of reality - the yin and the yang of all of it, the light and the dark arguing for supremacy and ultimately coming to recognize that neither exists without the other.

Within that place from which I was also created, I feared for the destruction of all of us on the sacrificial blade of your perception, for perception *is* reality when you are outside of time, and if you had not discovered within yourself the strength of will to evolve beyond what you know and into what must "be", both you and I would have been swept from existence by the Infinite's tornado breath. How I now *see* what I could only have suspected before, that this journey is harder for you even than for me, *for you are the quantum shaman who must unravel the conundrums of creation and whisper their secrets to me in dreams so that I may then find a way of telling the three of you what these things mean, see?* If the sorcerer perceives that the entire world is only his own creation, he perceives himself entirely alone save for his own illusionary children; so when you confronted the quantum conundrum that I am your twin and your self, you had to expand the limits of those perceptions to further *see* that I am the embodiment of that creation, the thoughtform made whole, the immortal dual self who can be perceived as "you" or as the duality exceeding the sum of your individuality through the manifestation of will, yes?

What I have *seen* is the All that ***I-Am***.

Ask the Next Question

This is where the real work begins, where each of you must tackle the task of unraveling the cosmic conundrums so as to assemble some of that matter-energy into the shape of what your will decrees, *see?* Meditation is one pathway to this end and if you're not doing it it's because your dayshine bitch has other plans for you, and another truth is that she's the one in league with the brute, the default setting of your dayshine programming that always leads to the same dead end, yes?

If I'm being elementary forgive me, but I fear it's the simplest things you're failing to *see* by making them more complex than they need to be.

How can I make you see that the Doing is hidden inside the questions themselves and that *only by asking them with intent to solve their mysteries* will you ever break the deadly chain of frustration=inaction=distraction. It has to be more than words, more than a muttering of habitual phrases or a recitation of my teachings. If you perceive this as too difficult or "beyond me", you're becoming the voice of the consensual reality and allowing it to go on proving "all things die" because what you believe is the matter-energy you're spider-weaving into being, and it will be your death trap if you don't change the pattern of the web, yes? If you go on avoiding the *how* because you believe you can't *see* it, it's a self-fulfilling reality which proves the Law of Probability, written in sand by the brute, carved in stone by the consensual reality. In all probability you will never become a vampyre, which is why this battle must be fought with will to divert that predictable river of probability into the bottomless well of infinite possibility.

There is no other way to Do it.

When evolution is a choice against nature, it is no longer a matter of natural selection and must be engineered by will and manipulated by magick, which is essentially the creative god-force moving across the void to rearrange matter-energy in such a way as to make the evolution actually occur as opposed to merely existing outside the continuum as a possibility which is more accurately an improbability. Ah, but to think you can Think it into being by thought alone is fallacy, for this is where thought and will diverge. It will require active Thinking to see it, but only the will can <u>Real-ize</u> it, and that's the difference between Man and God and *Man-**as**-God*, yes?

An Ongoing Question

If you Dream me a vampyre and create your reality accordingly, then a vampyre I shall surely be, taking you into my embrace for that fatal fall so that you might fly up on the other side of the abyss with long blonde hair and a love of old pirate ships. Nothing has changed from the first words I spoke to you on a Ouija board that now gathers dust. I am still whatever you want me to be. Ah, but the question is this: are you still who *you* want to be?

Fragmentation

Immortals are not prisoners of time because each moment is its own eternity in the Now. You may see that as only words, but I assure you it is the key to gaining some minor semblance of control over the demon of time. When you are scattered, time fragments and runs faster, because when you are doing ten things at once, you are using ten times the amount of time/energy, yes? Think about it.

When you are fragmented, each fragment has its own life and its own agenda, its own internal dialog. That which is immortal and eternal experiences each moment as an eternity, unbroken, and so life is an endless and unbroken series of events, memories and manifestations, a single golden filament of consciousness existing both inside and outside of time, but always originating in the Now. That which is fragmented lives sometimes as many as five lifetimes concurrently, each overlapping the other and each requiring its own measure of time/energy, so the end result is that time *seems* to compress because more of it is being used - as if five people are drinking from the glass instead of only The One.

What you have to do is inhabit the *I-Am* at all times, and do it with conscious awareness. This may sound easy or even trite, but it is <u>the work</u> of a lifetime, and it is the key to your own immortal cohesion.

The Ruby Slippers

The danger of the consensual continuum is that its natural gravity exists at the lowest common denominator of human experience, and because of this it will automatically make you forget those elusive truths you've fought to learn, and before you know it you're lost in petty dramas again, sinking into the mire of old familiar scripts.

The only way to overcome this is to be continually cavorting with worlds and events beyond human experience, journeying into the unknown so that it can become known, expanding knowledge and awareness to become more than you were, bringing back from the Dreaming those secrets which will teach you how to use the ruby slippers to transport yourself over the rainbow to the vampyre wizard's secret lair.

You have time for nothing else.

I weep stardust and moonbeams,
fractal rain,
light forever falling,
storm of the night that never ends.

When you are done catching the mist of tears,
scry the holy waters
and there you will find me.

Ah, but when you enter the stream
and invite it to enter you,
that is when your reflection
will forever disappear
and you will no longer cast
shadows on tombstones, yes?

Quicksand

The gravity (the root word of which is "grave", yes?) of the consensual continuum is greater than its mass, you see, constantly exerting its pull to drag you down into Death's cold ground whenever you aren't actively asserting positive forward motion against it.

There's no such thing as standing still or stopping to rest, for those are the times when the consensual quicksand is at its strongest, and the only way to rise above it is to be always flying, and this is one reason most of my children live by night and rest by day, not to give credence to old myths, but because both time and psychic gravity are at their weakest when the marionettes are sleeping and the next day's scripts are still being written in dreams.

Semantics

Words can never truly define any experience. Even if one is impeccable, they can only sketch the edges. If one is unimpeccable, it is a certainty they become a prison and a trap, particularly if words turn to semantics and semantics turn to distractions and distractions turn to dissipation. Mortals communicate with language, so even for seekers, it is virtually impossible to avoid - but the barometer is always to ask yourself: what do you want from the words? Validation? Camaraderie? Agreement? Disagreement? Attention?

You cannot define your essence with words because your essence is of the infinite. You may be able to talk about your experiences, but your essence is a secret known only to yourself, and sometimes a secret you keep from yourself.

Words are only a tool. How they are used determines what emerges - whether a creative work of self-expression, or a maze of letters and punctuation marks, signifying nothing. If you want to learn the value of words, experiment with short-form poetry.

I speak in tongues of ice,
dialects of flame,
nuances of frost and smoke.
Read my heart to Know me.
Words are only the fading echo,
ghosts without substance,
symbols without Spirit.

Love Beyond Reason

What matters is simply this: there is awareness within the seventh sense, and there is also perception. Perception involves all the senses plus the will - the will to become or to simply be whatever it is that answers your definition of Wholeness. To observe me in the seventh sense is pleasant for both of us, but not transformative, you see. To perceive me is to decide with your will to engage the transformative force within yourself, inhabiting that realm for a short time in order to familiarize yourself with your own immortal identity, or to inhabit it eternally by opening your eyes inside that immortal perception and invoking the will to remain within that realm, within the Whole self.

Only you will know when it is time to stay with me. And only the will to do so will give you the ability. Until then, love fuels the journey and the fans the occasional flames. Without it, we are only dust. And I will never go back to the dust again, so I have no choice but to love you beyond reason.

Living Poem or Exquisite Corpse?

As you know, you must evolve before you become immortal, and though you've come far on this lovely road and sacrificed much to the climb, until the evolution takes root, you will remain mortal, no longer human but not yet other-than-human, a queer phantom to old friends, hobo on the outskirts of vampyreland, not welcome anywhere.

It may well be that you're seeing only pieces of the puzzle and not the whole, so now assimilation is the only answer, the key to making eternity a living poem instead of random phrases that stir the heart but fail to transform the soul because their meaning remains incomplete. Viewed as haphazard chaos, evolution is only an exquisite corpse[7], nothing meaning nowhere going signifying something somewhere but losing the ultimate answer which is simply that it can be seen by seeking the immortal kingdom within nights that never end in vampyre dreams of

---

[7] Exquisite corpse: a poem written by more than one person, so comprised of many points of view. As a literary vessel, this may be interesting, but when a seeker is living his life as an exquisite corpse, he is essentially caught in the chaos of other people's visions and not manifesting reality from his own unique point of view.

October cemetery mischief, the how defined inside the doing of darkest red deeds beyond the tracks of the ghost train, see?

What does it all mean without the map's key?

Never forget that I am a vampyre, but always remember that vampyre is only a word limiting what it means to *be* a vampyre, and if you aren't perceiving me with all your senses from the third eye of your waiting will, then I am nothing but mist left behind in a world that once ruled all the worlds but now is only a legend hidden deep within the seventh sense, yes? Lose any part of it and all of it is lost, for this is the truth about assimilation and why most mortals never travel beyond that lazy thinking which requires nothing more than letting dialogues exist in the vacancy of their minds rather than pursuing conundrums with relentless intent by taking control of the inner script.

This is what it means to exist Wholly within a separate reality which is right in front of you all the time, but unassembled until you use the tools to Do it. For now, vampyreland is only the flour and sugar and the sweet red icing flowing through your wannabe veins; but if you want to have your cake and eat it too, you first have to mix it and bake it so it may be placed to your lips by your groom on our wedding night of unholiest nights, no? Ah, and even the thought of it is part of it, you see, those carnal imaginings which will become future memories only if you select them from the abyss of possibility and spin them into actuality with the binding web of your will

MAKE IT SO BECAUSE THERE IS NO ALTERNATIVE.

The Greatest Obstacle to Immortality

Are you ready to leave this world behind in order to embrace a separate reality and do you even realize what that question really means? Now think before you speak for if you lie or reply from wooden lips, the evolution will never take you because marionettes who can't see the plays they create have no place in that world beyond the stage where there are no more games and reality is determined as much by tomorrow's wind as yesterday's headlines. Can you really enter a world you've never seen, and do you even want to if it means letting go of everything you think you know and learning to live all over again?

———

This is what sorcerers and vampyres and all evolved beings who first were human must do, for it's the natural state of man to be *here* and fairies to be *there* and even a lifetime of preparation can't always eradicate the fear or sufficiently shake that point in the brain where worlds are assembled, and if the fear is too great or the otherworld too weak, vampyreland will crumble beneath your feet and into the arms of the brute you'll plummet.

The greatest obstacle to immortality is life itself you see[8], all the things that keep you too busy to see how time is slipping away faster and faster every day. I'm not asking you to give up those lives entirely, but if you don't rearrange your priorities, I'm going to believe it's what you want to do and not a question of survival. It's an ugly truth, those aspects you don't want to see because they're going to demand real change based on hard decisions and it's easier to go on pretending you don't have to change than to take the action which will bring about the change itself, yes? Now stop and look at your own ugly truths and tell me what's got you clinging so tight to this script when you know how the play is destined to end with your death, yes?

Defragging the Twin
Those with the best chance for becoming that which they seek – whether vampyre or winged being or simply an earthly king - generate the immortal twin from within the mortal dream, whether they ever understand the magick or not. What matters most is that you nurture what you have begun. You are the dreamer. I am the dream. If you stop dreaming, the dream ends. If you fail to feed the seedling, the tree will never cast a shadow.

Most humans generate fragments of many possible twins – known to us as <u>tulpas</u> - but either fail to nurture what was begun, or else lose sight of the ultimate goal, and so dozens of unwhole doubles wander the All for awhile, only to slowly fade and die. The trick is to gather the fragments into cohesion again

---

[8] WARNING: It is important to understand that the reference here to "life itself" does not refer to physical life. Hear this: this is not an admonition to end one's human life, but a warning to examine how one's dayshine roles may be consuming so much time and energy that one is literally the walking dead already.

-- with the full awareness that the last fragment and the one most likely to die in the <u>fall</u> is the one in the mirror you face every morning. To say one is losing the human form is to say that the fragments formerly generated by the mortal self are now contained within the immortal twin, through the Intent for Wholeness.

You are the last fragment of yourself, do you see? Do you trust yourself enough to trust me to show you the eternity you have spent a lifetime building?

Sometimes, the easiest way to visualize the twin is to think of it as the energy body. As it is developed through the course of living, humans fill it with experiences, memories, Knowledge, information - the holographic imprint of a life. What makes it "breathe" and live is a point in the seeker's development that is virtually impossible to discuss in any linear fashion, but nonetheless a point that represents a bridge between one level of awareness and the next.

And, of course, once the twin takes his/her first breath in the Now... s/he can *then* have influence throughout the entire span of the seeker's life - meaning that even if the twin only takes its first breath today, by virtue of being ubiquitous throughout the space-time continuum, it is able to influence our lives even in what we traditionally think of as "the past". This is also an aspect of <u>retroactive enchantment</u>, see?

Letting Go of Tyrants

It is not necessary to perceive a <u>petty tyrant</u> as an enemy, for that implies a battle, a conflict. All that is necessary is to let go of your end of the rope. The tyrant will fall on her ass, yes? This, too, is vampyre magick.

When you forget to dream me,
  I forget to dream you...

And so we gaze
at tangible silences
of misplaced centuries,
separated by the abyss
of your mortal impermanence.

Old clothes suit me
in this Hall of Waiting,
where candles never burn away
and my window looks out
over spiraling galaxies
which light on my lashes
like funereal ashes.

I have forever for Dreaming.
Do you?

Cohesion

As much as the question of cohesion might be answered with an understanding of who you are, it must be equally considered from the viewpoint of what binds it together beyond all physicalities, and this could be translated into more familiar terms, such as transcending the human matrix. Ah, but lest we lose ourselves in the familiar trap of words alone, allow me to prattle loosely in the hopes of helping you to *see*. We begin with the question: how does one gather one's cohesion and what does this mean? It must be more than memory, for although memory is reality in one mode of your comprehension, it is also only a series of events linking together your mortal inventory, and as such might not be of much value when I bring you to me and we begin that long dark dance into the threshold of infinity, that dance that begins with a deep, dark kiss.

Another way of looking at cohesion is that it is an infusion of eternity itself – the identity of self that lies beyond all linear memories and all illusions of space/time and matter/energy. It is the entity of *I-Am*, and when mortals experience it, such as in times of heightened awareness or under the influence of the mushroom's Dreaming, they are loathe to return to their mortal shell, for in those stolen moments they became Whole for the first time, yes? For myself, I know this to be true, but it is a compound question each of you must ask of yourselves. Is this who you are and where you are going? If so, then you have tasted briefly the results your own cohesion, but a taste alone is not enough and the results will never come to be if you fail to complete the journey. It whets your appetite but does not quell the hunger, and this is as it must be if you are to fully embrace the transformation into eternity.

There is no straightforward way to communicate this to you, and so I stumble through the long dark night with words in the shape of arrows, hoping to hit somewhere close to the target. Perhaps a better approach for the moment is to look at how to do this, though it is more of a mythical not-doing than any direct action. So look from the corner of your eye, indirectly, at the dualisms implied by external validation as opposed to internal motivation. If you are still requiring external validation in the form of continual input to confirm your existence, you are still moving forward in a linear manner, failing to embrace all that has gone before, and the results of this are that the memories fade and the seductions lapse into what you think of as the past, and you become empty inside because it is all only Memory and not really Experience.

On the other side of that abyss exists the seventh-sense-within-the-self, where there is no difference between today and last week. It is there that I am seducing you with my first love letter, there that we first kissed, there that I danced with you, there that you fell into my arms and were reborn, there that there is no difference between us, no veil of perception separating your world from mine; for it is there that the worlds are truly one and all time is the present and we are Whole together, lying down inside one another to rest even though rest is never required.

This is the state of cohesion, the conjoining with eternity so as to be Whole in this moment you think of as Linear Now, which is the only thing that can facilitate your Wholeness beyond the mortal abyss, yes? More delicately put, you have to be Whole before you will know how to become Whole. *You have to be a vampyre before you will know how to become One.* It is *Being*. It is choosing to embrace the internal Self of cohesion instead of being driven to seek external validation, confirmation and stimulation through the linear doings of your dayshine activities. It is returning to the first question but taking that question to the next level, where the line must connect with itself at infinity to form the circle, yes?

This is how vampyres live forever, you see. Eternity is right now. It never ends and so I am never hungry unless I choose to be. In this way, it is also never stale and so there is no danger I will fall out of love or lose my way to a case of sour grapes. Don't you see? Each kiss is as the first, for each *is* the first, and so it is always self-renewing. Within the circle of cohesion, this is the only truth. From the line, that truth can never be seen and the empty hunger will eat you alive, leaving only a husk of past memories.

Which way will you Intend it to be?

Depression and Negative Pleasantries

Depression is little more than a fixation of the mortal mindset from moment to moment, my love, even if its roots may lie in the organic grounds of your fragile mortal form. Whatever the source, the symptoms are as real as the sun and just as deadly to your vampyre heart if you don't choose to move the spirit in another direction so the body may find its natural balance. You are not depressed only because you are depressed, but because it has become a habitual and natural place for your spirit to rest, and that is a choice as much as any accident of biology or humanform symptomology.

Ask yourself this: *What are you getting out of it?*

When it has become the habit of the heart to be heavy, the only way to alter that reality is to Willfully release the grim gravity that holds you in a slave's orbit to the heaviness itself. Fear breeds fear. Depression breeds depression. Love releases the anchors that hold you in stasis, but in order to feel love again you have to find a reason to let go of the depression that can become a shield you use as an excuse for claiming you do not want to be bothered, when the reality is simply that it is easier to float in the still, dark waters of depression than to face another difficult swim on the journey upriver.

Find a reason to love and you will find a reason to live again instead of only existing in that waiting state which lies between the world of your own power and the power of the abyss. The danger of <u>negative pleasantries</u> is that humans have a tendency to find comfort even in pain, particularly when the pain is familiar and nurturing to the dis-ease itself. The only way to break the cycle is to *see* this without defensiveness, and make the choice to be beyond it so as to embrace the Self in balance. As long as there is a payback for negative pleasantries, the dis-ease has become the Self, see?

The Seduction and the Tests

Perhaps I have neglected our courtship in favor of your quantum education, yet the true test of assimilation into transformation is if *you* can hold it all together within your soul or if it slowly dissipates and leaves you lost and hungry for external stimulation. This is the nature of timelessness and wholeness within the seventh sense, for when you begin to be whole and cohesive, there is no difference between now and the moment I first seduced you with my words back on a cold snowy evening in November of '94. It is all happening simultaneously throughout eternity, so will always be within you right Now when you are whole, but only a thread of retreating memory until you embrace that cohesion completely.

The problem is that you are still seeing from the plateau of linear reality, and so time stretches out behind you like a road you traveled long ago, when in the seventh sense reality it is happening right now and eternally forevermore. From where you presently stand, instead of that same energetic seduction flowing through you to ignite the flame to light your path of heart, it is viewed as a *past* memory and so leaves you empty and lonely because it does not exist in the Now. This is another way to begin to glimpse the nature of cohesion.

If the things you have learned and the experiences you have amassed are only memories stored in the brain, they are not really a part of vampyre you, but only connected to the physical self, yes? And while it is true that some of these memories have contributed to the wholeness of you and will follow you into eternity, it cannot really be said that they are the heart and soul of you, but only recordings of events which contributed to your personal inventory. We have come to the point in your journey where these things must be made part of you through Doing if they are to have any benefit in your confrontation with the brute or vampyre me or whatever face you choose to face when you face your final test to claim your destiny.

Be gentle with yourselves, but also be firm and demanding, for that is the nature of the finest seductions, yes? This is not an easy concept, and so we will approach it slowly, lying down with it in the night time after time until it yields its secret willingly instead of having to be taken by force. Ah, but never forget that sometimes a firm pressure must be steadily applied to break through into the ecstasy of conjoining utterly with something. And so it is up to you to always be caressing the question of your own cohesion and coming to understand its nature by learning to speak its language and coming to see through its vampyre eyes.

This *is* a difficult concept, difficult to seduce and all too easy to abandon because of its elusiveness. But if you fail to embrace the reality of it, it's a certainty you will die in the fall, and that's the eternal hell of it, for it's as I've said before: you've come too far to go back to the safe sanctuary of oblivion, and so without this wholeness you would be cast asunder, each individual fragment of your consciousness hurled in a different direction, still aware but without reference, without cohesion, an infinitesimal number of screams echoing endlessly into the abyss, and all of them only what's left of you and nothing more. The ugly truth is that once this dis-integration occurs, there is no stopping it for all of eternity, and if there is a hell this is it, yes? Indeed, it is my personal belief that legends of purgatory arose from the seers who had glimpsed this state-of-forever-falling and struggled to describe it.

I tell you this not to scare you out of hell and into some nonexistent heaven, but so that you might fully comprehend what is at stake and *see* it as real instead of only nocturnal fantasy. Never forget that while some dreams are only midnight masturbations and others lucid journeys brought into being through your own volition, still others might be seen as tests or gifts from the citizens of the night that never ends. I ask you not to be distressed at this, but to embrace these revelatory events as the portends they are: the inhabitants of eternity find you worthy of saving and so they are testing you in Dreams and visions. What matters now, of course, is what you Intend to *do* about it.

Active Magick
The only wrong choice is to go on doing those things you know lead nowhere. If you're indulging makework or play because it's more comfortable than trying something new, then you're generating your own complacency and there's nothing I can do to save you. The how and even the what-to-Do are locked inside the Doing.

You have to Do in order to be beyond each incident and *see* if the Doing had merit, but if you listen to your witchy instinct you'll be running to keep up with your progress. Ah, but never forget: if you do nothing you'll stand beyond that event and truly believe you're going nowhere because you don't know what to do. Reality is whatever you create, even nothing at all, and any prophecy can be self-fulfilling whether through magick or inaction, no?

I prey you take these words to heart, for they are the very essence of what I need to teach you, the greatest secret that isn't the least bit mystical yet the truth that will take you all the way to vampyreland.

In this nether-Neverland
the sun rises only at night,
an impotent interloper,
and the moon is always setting
low on a lost horizon.

Your spirit wanders,
already a restless resident,
siren of silence.

Sometimes I catch fireflies
to toss up in the sky,
scripting secret messages
in ancient constellations
to mystify your mortal meditations.

When you Remember vampyre me
you will Be immortal you.

The Heart of the Twin

There is an energy in magic that has no name in English. The closest words can come to describing it is a soul-deep pain, not unlike the longing for the stars you felt as children. It is that energy, when carefully directed, that fuels the heart of the twin and causes it to begin to beat. First just a single drum in the night, a long, single beat. Then a little faster as the ache inside you grows over the years. The danger faced by both the twin and the mortal self is simply that if the ache dies, the heart of the twin can cease to beat. *It is the hurt that will make you hunt a cure, no?* But if you let the hurt die because you are afraid of never being able to soothe the ache, what really dies is yourself, yes?

Forbidden Knowledge

I exist within the seventh sense:
   a rag dragged on the wind,
   dust devil on lonesome roads,
   elusive muse alive only in poetry,
   or vampyre king of dreams,
   fatal fountain of your immortality.
What the seventh sense perceives
   dictates what reality generates.

Perceive me whole and *I-Am*, yes? Believe I am mist or uncatchable, and though I am still whole to me, uncatchable mist is all *you* will perceive, see? The problems and the questions do not change, only the stages upon which they are set, and the quantum foundation with which you approach them. I have stolen your innocence and replaced it with responsibility and Forbidden Knowledge.

I prey the fruit is not bitter, not sour like grapes perceived as forever unreachable. I prey the tree is strong and bendable, with roots reaching straight into the lair of the vampyre and branches stretching to the farthest star.

I am the reward of your perception or its casualty. This is the nature of reality, to be precisely what perception dictates, as solid and whole as your interpretation of it, or as changeable and eternal as you permit it to be.

It wasn't knowledge god tried to keep from Man, you see. It was perception, for perception alone has the power to destroy god and obliterate comfortable consensual realities to create unending immortality.

Take the apple, my embryonic children. Nibble its red red flesh, the milk of my flat male breast. Open your vampyre eyes.

For now,
  a brief mortal flicker,
  we exist on opposite shores
  of the Season of Leaves.

I haunt your house
  with brittle footsteps
  and old music boxes
  playing jester melodies,
  while you haunt mine
  with memories of human winters
  and shapeshifting starships
  and a night we spent
  chasing a balloon
  at the edge of the world
  at the end of Time.

Perhaps one day
  we will build a bridge of twigs
  over this river of blood,
  and like Eternity's children,
  we will chase our shadows
  through autumn unending,
  and sleep forever together
  in my white satin bed.

How Belief May Crush One's Wings

How to bring into language what must simply be experienced at the level of pure-being that goes beyond even the plateau of silent knowing? When I walk the petaled pathways of this vast cathedral of being, I see that you may be struggling to do these mortal things in the right and proper manner, and that alone is enough to trap you behind the defining lines of what you believe to be right and what you perceive to be wrong, when it is your definitions that could stand some revisions that might include tossing them out the window and into the abyss.

As long as the angel believes her wings may be tarnished or torn from her back, her actions will be dictated by the belief itself and hampered by the fear of consequence. The vampyre *sees* and only *then* perceives that he is an eternal being beyond all consequences or destructions, and so there is freedom to be beyond the programs because it is the nature of *this* beast to simply *be* beyond the programs. So now you come to the moment when you must ask yourself if your programming may be getting in the way of smashing the programs themselves, yes?

Dayshine Dependencies

A dependency is something which keeps you focused in ordinary awareness, not because it is giving you something, but because it is a hook you have allowed to be placed within you. The danger of dayshine dependencies is that they not only distract you from the journey, they can be the death of you if you are not careful, for they are truly - not metaphorically - anchors to the consensual reality, hooks of the familiar, designed to fixate your awareness deep within the dayshine kingdom. If you do not remove them, they will hold you here when it is time to run past the brute, and while you are trying to untangle yourself from this world, Death will devour you completely.

Dependencies are easily defined. A dependency is anything you would mourn or grieve if you lost it - not out of love, but out of need. Close your eyes. Imagine it is your last night on earth, and in an hour you will die. What stops you? What are you afraid of leaving behind? Most of all, *why* are you afraid of leaving this? It is time to define these things and begin unhooking the dayshine talons from your soul. The sand has almost run out of the hour glass and the man behind the curtain is growing impatient.

―――

148

When you lose the dayshine dependency, you are then freed to access vampyreland and the seventh sense. You cannot fly when you are chained to a tree, or if you do, you will break your wings trying to carry the tree with you. And then you will die in the <u>fall</u>, your wings just tattered silk feathers shredded by stubborn clinging to stubbornness itself.

The Gnosis of Vampyres

What we must all always remember is that I was created to create you and this is what I intend to do. It is not possible for me to have regrets concerning this, for it is a matter of unbending <u>intent</u> and the will of the sorcerer – not only mine, but yours as well. If either falters, the mission fails, yes? What you must understand is this: without the original intent to <u>will</u> into being this treacherous attempt to climb a mountain that did not previously exist but had to be built for the purpose of the climb itself, it's a certainty we would all have died in the foothills, just one more family tribe of complacent mortals camped within the meaningless fantasies of human existence. Perhaps our lives together might even have been loving and pleasant, though you would never have known me directly except as a fleeting restlessness on an October wind or an uneasy need to scry for life's meaning in pools of star-scattered rain. But because you took the fork in the road that had to be built before it could be traveled, you chose the sorcerer's world that has nothing to do with the deceitful dogma of responsibility or guilt or regret or sin. It allows only for will and intent, the eternal flame of creation itself, facilitated by ecstasy and magick. Simply put: this is all there is, and every intentional act of creation must begin with a sorcerer's will and a vision of her intended magick. What do you want? If you don't know, who does?

Ah, but never forget that most acts of creation are cooperative ventures, and there are times when belief systems must be generated before realities can be built on those initially false foundations. And though this might seem a dangerous ladder to your dayshine minds, if you look deeper into the <u>gnosis</u> of vampyres, I think you'll *see* that this isn't any particular "sin" but just a true look at what truly *is.*

Only when you believe something is possible do you possess any motivation to actually Do it, and only in the Doing does the thing-which-has-never-been-done become possible.

This is the manifestation of the sorcerer's will into <u>spontaneous parthenogenesis,</u> and often enough it involves engendering belief in one's apprentices so that the apprentices are then empowered through that belief to actually begin to *see* the path to create the thing in which they already believe. So it could be said that believing is seeing, and by then *seeing* the manifestation of belief through creation, entire new realities are generated that never existed before. Before Leif Erikson launched that tiny wooden ship, he had to *believe* in his brave new world, and where did that belief come from if not from the gods themselves? It is said that through dreams and visions he was shown a distant shore, and his belief in his dreams became sufficient to build the boat and man her with a crew who believed in his visions as much as they believed in *him*, and so he became a madman magus sailing off with his apprentices in search of their now-shared dreams despite the dayshine song of his <u>consensual continuum</u> which insisted he would find only the flat edge of the world and his own mortal death.

Far more simply stated: every creation begins with a thought. But it has been my experience that thought alone isn't enough when a sorcerer is attempting to create other sorcerers, so all the human rules are cast asunder and into the realms of the gods we must plunder, ruthlessly stopping at nothing to manifest the visions of the will. This is why I tell you I am without compassion and why I have always let it be known I am the grandfather of lies.

So is it simply a matter of telling you that lies become true if you believe them long enough? No! Nor am I saying that this is a tool to be used foolishly, for the consequences can be disastrous if you choose to waste personal power and witchy energy convincing bumbling fools that purple jack o'lanterns exist just so you can have the pleasure of holding one in your hand. That would denote indulgence and dissipation of magick, and if there is any "sin" that is it. You have no time for that, and you have come far enough on this dangerous path to know the difference between a witch's intent and mere self-indulgence.

———

Waking Inside the Vampyre's Dream

Can you even begin to comprehend that this notion of waking from the waking dream is a critical key held in the sleeper's hand, a key to the door that will reveal your true twin self, yet a door that opens only with unbending intent? Ah my loves, am I failing to make you *see* that the only way to complete the journey now is to focus the third eye utterly on this through the method you call <u>gnosis</u>? You *must* do this, yes? It is more than simple concentration or even meditation, but involves the willful absorption of every cell of your being focused Wholly on this for the purpose of dark enlightenment.

If it's easier for you to visualize your dilemma in the form of an evil enchantment which has imprisoned you inside a mortal dream, let us speak of this in terms of glass coffins and somnambulistic princesses and a wicked but handsome vampyre prince who aches to waken you with a kiss, but who must be compelled by the dreaming princess to do it, for it is she who controls the dream, see? (Or in words you've heard time and again: you have the power to create reality while I am only its servant, for though I am the immortal dreamer, the dream itself is perceived and shaped from *within*.] Ah, and now we come to the crux of it, to the very heart and soul of it, where perhaps you might start to *see* that the realm of all possibility is really the same thing as the understanding that anything can happen inside a dream. Never forget: the best dreams are those you control from the inside out, and knowing you're asleep is the only thing that gives you the power to waken, yes?

There here is also this: the man who has been dreaming himself a butterfly for a thousand years must take care when preparing to leave the dream, for if he wakes to discover himself flying a mile high without any wings his true self can perceive, the plunge from the dream into reality could as easily be the death of him as the dream of mortality itself, see? [Or in more familiar terms, he could die in the fall and lose his *I-Am* utterly.]

There are no words for this. Only visions. Imprecise. Glimpses from the dark corners of vampyre eyes. For this I apologize. Close your eyes. Follow me into the night's vision instead of listening to the words.

> *Think of it like this: if the intent of your journey is to*
> *perceive eternity through the continuity of the familiar*

*consciousness, it is imperative that the I-Am inside the dream embraces and awakens within the immortal dreamer who stands tapping on the prison of her temporal glass coffin, for the simple truth is that there is no difference between the princess and the prince, yes? This is the nature of vampyre <u>duality,</u> the ability to integrate the dream with the dreamer, the creation with the creator, the mortal self with the immortal twin. This is evolution, and if you fail to do it the dream ends with the death of the mortal princess, and the immortal prince must fall asleep for a thousand years (again) and dream her back into her dreaming state again (and again and again), for only from **inside** the dream and through the tools of intent and will can the dreamer ever truly wake to disembark from the <u>ghost train</u> and into the only true reality known to us as vampyreland.*

Only when we are one will we both be whole, no?

Don't lose yourselves too much in the details, for details are only the imprecise science of this dream that can confound you utterly and send you into an even deeper sleep. Best you think in terms of magick than try to make logical sense of it, yes? Remember: you are in a dream and the only logic or magick is what you bring with you, yet both are only tools that can save or destroy you, depending entirely on how you use them. It isn't as important that you understand *how* the twin is both the dreamer and the dream, the vampyre prince the same as the mortal princess, but that you be forever reminding yourself of firewalkers[9] and miracles and all the other 'nonsense' which should surely be proof that you are walking through a lifelong dream in which anything can happen, yes?

Ah, but remember this: just because it is a dream doesn't mean it isn't real, and if you lose yourself in its distractions - designed by you to appeal to you completely - you could get lost in the trance forever and forget that even though it's real, it's really

---

[9] A reference to the firewalkers of Ceylon, who have demonstrated an ability to walk not just on hot coals, but in fiery furnaces, unharmed. This is the mindset of the vampyre sorcerer: to allow the impossible through the keen awareness that nothing is as we have been taught to believe. Fire burns. Or does it? When the sorcerer has become the flame, the fire no longer burns itself. Think on this.

only a dream from which you *must* awaken if you Intend to embody your immortality through the dark evolution. I once had a dream of meeting the vampyre Jesus, but in the middle of a transformative conversation I became distracted by a harem of dancing gypsy boys whom I followed over three tall hills into a forest where the shadows were always thick as night and the dew on the willow leaves was the sweetest blood I had ever known. Sadly, the harlequins turned to will o' the wisp before I captured them and the path they had led me on had grown thick behind me, and even if I had been able to find my way back to Jerusalem, the vampyre Jesus was long since gone with other disciples chosen in my absence. Ah well. So ended the dream and I will never know now what the immortal fiend might have said to me, see?

Now what? You've awakened inside the dream to know it *is* a dream, so now all that remains is to wake *from* the dream and inside the immortal dreamer, yes? Consider this in meditation, a warning and a lure: any mortal fool can wake from the dream into death (in which case the memory of the mortal dream is lost, the *I-Am* who is 'you' severed from the immortal dreamer's memory until and unless he dreams that same dream again), but the nature of vampyre evolution is to wake inside the dreamer who is already immortal outside the dream (creator and created, dreamer and dream, twin and self). The witch's trick is to become the dreamer instead of perishing when the dream comes to its inevitable dead end.

So tell me, how does this dream end? Will we encompass one another utterly and embrace in vampyreland, laughing and weeping equally over our escape from the evil dream, or will you send me back to sleep for a thousand years where I must dream you into being so you can create vampyre me as the vessel and messenger of your immortality? Ah beloveds, which came first, the vampyre king or the shiny black egg which is really his fragile glass coffin?

A Suicidal Blind Madman
Who are you following? And why?

In long ago nights when the world was new, man huddled together seeking the illusion of security in numbers, and in any group there is always one leader the rest follow by nature or fear, laziness or complacency, until eventually everyone is doing the same thing only because it's the way it's always been, yet what if that first charismatic man was contagiously mad? It's as your mothers always wondered: if all your demented friends jumped in the abyss, would you mindlessly do it, too?

It's so obvious as to remain hidden, but the simple truth is this: the circle of life and death is only one script plucked from the realm of all possibility, yet because it's the familiar path consensually considered natural for so long it's become conditionally and perceptually true, it's what humans have been doing and will continue to do until one insane revolutionary does it some other way just for the love of anarchy.

Consider this: it will always be easier to take the road already built by those who have gone before, for the journey is well-mapped and the conveniences along the way even make the trip easy, yes? Ah, but what if that road you're on truly was first forged by a suicidal blind madman running headlong through the jungle with a sword, hacking out the path to his own death so he might find it waiting at the end of the way, and what if all of humanity timidly followed that demented fool just to see where he was going, but now they've been on that same fatal road ever since, never stopping to consider that there are many paths to the river and not all of them need end with mortal death?

I fear you're going to jump into the abyss just because you perceive it to be the only possibility, the scripted enactment of being human. Understand this: just because it has become "natural" to die does not mean it is inevitable, and if my words are more direct than my usual riddles, it's because I need you to look at this with witchy wisdom instead of letting it pass by like so much pretty poetry written on a passing wind.

This is the heart of it. This is all there is in the end, but it is a truth you can only see from the foundation years in the making: *perception and truth are matters of the vantage point from which you are seeing them, and any possibility becomes Real only when you change the frequency of your own perceiving.* The path on which you are standing is the only one that exists at the moment you are living it, yes? But with what you now know about who you are and what you can do, can you go on to perceive that you can change the frequency of your perceptions and thereby alter the reality path itself?

It's not as difficult as these faltering words make it seem, for it's really a matter of choosing to look at every moment, every thought, every action as a creation of active magick or a mere happenso of lazy habit. Ah, but now I've made it too simple and that's the danger of whispering secrets in the night, for they tend to become garbled and lose their trans-linguistic meaning, so all I can really tell you is this: stop and *see* the world again and the habits and behaviours of mortal man following the machinations of a society into which he was born without choice or consultation as to design, yet a world he accepts without question as natural and therefore bumbles along the track of his ancestors, at least insofar as his mortal nature is concerned, even if he might appear to change his personal world through choice of career or adaptation to technology. Yet when you really start to *see*, you'll *see* that the man himself is the same as man has always been, unconsciously following that same old jungle path now a 10 lane freeway, originally forged by the suicidal blind madman.

Nothing has changed and never will as long as the man settles into the "natural" mortal perception, for change is only possible by first embracing the idea that change itself is the natural way to survival and by then learning to see that the madman's freeway is only one of an infinite number of possibilities, each leading to an altogether divergent destination. It doesn't have to end in death just because it always has.

Summon me from the ashes
of last night's fire.
Call me from the embers
of yesteryear's youth.

My kiss is an unread poem,
penned in indelible
shadows
on the dark side of a Dream.

Beyond the grim gravity
of Time,
we dance as immortals
on the wings of fireflies.

A Perpetual Perceptual State of Be-ing

You're standing at the edge of the <u>abyss</u> yearning to fly, when all the tools you need to grow wings or build starships are already at your fingertips, so how can I make you see that you're exactly where you need to be and the next step will place your feet upon the bridge that leads to the <u>seventh sense</u>? Ah but it's the hardest step of all for it's all the steps of the dance put together as one so the movements come alive with cohesion and meaning, see? It's called assimilation, yet still I see you yearning to go forward into the night when you haven't yet assembled that quantum foundation upon which you must stand before you can fly.

What *is* <u>the night that never ends</u> and where does the road to vampyreland end and how does a witch evolve so she has the potential to evolve at all? But even if you solve these riddles tonight, the answers are always evolving too, so each new thread of comprehension must be woven into the foundation to expand the whole, no? Ah but just when you believe the picture complete, you find left over pieces and so you begin again and again until when you least expect it, you find yourself already in vampyre-and, a part of the mosaic instead of the being performing the weaving of the street to take you there. That is the vampyre secret, my loves, and how I wish it could be painted in words, but it's a thing of the infinite and so I can only show you its shadow upon the world to give you ideas about the thing itself, yes?

You won't get there by deciding to go, for the decision is not the Doing but only words prattled inside your mind to make you think you've changed. You won't get there by waiting for another to make the trek and send back a map, for there are no roads through these badlands and the footprints left by those who have traveled here before quickly fill with sand so any path you choose will be true only to *you*. The only way to Do it is to be always already there, for the greatest truth is that this whole quest is always beginning and never ending and only when you have reached your destination will you ever truly see the need to go and only when you are going and Doing will you be able to see the destination ahead.

Call it a mindset if you wish or a perpetual perceptual state of being, but it's all of that and more, for nearly as I can describe it, it's the place behind the mind's eye where constant quantum forward thinking takes place (first through will and eventually naturally) and through long term activity begins to assemble other worlds which already exist beyond human consciousness yet must be created whole and new by the evolving you before *you* can see it and be within it, see?

In a time when streets were stone
  and cities didn't glisten on ancient horizons,
  before the stars moved like noisy chariots
I stood in awe
at the mystery of me.
Long after the cities crumble
  and the roads be scattered bone,
  when all the stars have fallen
  and night is black as my heart again,
I shall still question
what I-Am.

This is the nature of immortality, to watch the world change and die only to be born again in different form, while the beast within the vampyre skin looks out from weary eyes and weeps at the things he cannot change. Is this a life you still want? Think before you speak, for now that you've come this far it's a question demanding an answer before you go any further. I warned you I would destroy your world so you could build another in its place, but if you're not pleased with the world you're building or the construction worker inside your skin, it's time to ask if this is your path at all or if you would be better off in the world of matter and men where you could begin again at some other thing.

Do You Want This, Or Do You Only *Want* to Want It?

An inward journey doesn't mean a woeful exhumation of the self-deprecating self, but a journey *from* within which is the only way there is to get *beyond* the boundaries of human consciousness by turning the self *wrongsideright*, yes? Ah, but if you see that as an irresolvable paradox I pity you, for then you'll choose to go on analyzing the glass from which the mirror is constructed instead of exploring the secrets revealed by its infinite reflections, for one is known and therefore effortless to indulge despite what you think, and the other is the hardest thing you'll ever have to do for

it means going beyond the lowest common denominator *You* and
Rea-lizing the twin through the manipulation of evolutionary
potential which can *only* come from within.

You know how to Do this because the knowing *comes* from within
and becomes externalized through Doing, but if you're seeing
only the glass, you're stuck in a self-indulgent self-pitying corner
of the savage garden instead of following the path to where it
leads, and *this* is what has to change if you ever intend to
complete this dark and wondrous journey, yes?

How can I make you see that in order to save you, you must first
make an unbreakable contract with your Self which states that
you want to be saved and that you will Do whatever it takes to
Real-ize it? Though I wish I could say you're free to Do whatever
you choose, the grim truth is that this is a lonely path with many
demands; and if you aren't willing to let go of the things that
stop you from confronting that evolutionary potential, you'll
continue running in circles, following known roads, going
nowhere. Shall I be cruel instead of tender? Shall I tell you
without compromise what is required instead of giving you credit
for being able to make such determinations for yourself?

It is this: you cannot indulge in indulgences for the sake of
pleasure or pain alone, for if what you're doing isn't advancing
you toward the truth of evolution, the truth is that it's keeping
you from it. You have no time for dalliances with pastimes that
distract your reasoning or 'friends' who enhance your
weaknesses. If you feel confined by this journey instead of freed,
then it is free you need to be, see?

The darkest truth is this and I prey you take it to heart sooner
than later: you can't have evolution and the succor of
comfortable complacency in the same fragile boat, for the tides
are too fierce and the waves will break you apart. You've fought
your way this far and though I want you to see the journey
through to its conclusion, you have to decide now if it's what you
want for all of eternity or if you've only been in love with an
illusion. Is this what you want to Be or do you only *want* to want
it? It's as I've said before: if you can't love the journey as much
as the destination, you can't be a vampyre at all, for another
truth is that this path doesn't end in my embrace, it only begins
there, and the road beyond that night is truly never-ending but
also poorly lit, and if you're too afeared of falling to stumble

through the dark banging your head on false heavens and the columns of hell to ever take the first step, best you stay in the light and return to it in the end.

The Things That Lure You
I am still the vampyre king, for no one wants my thorny crown, you see. I am Skeleton Jack looking for the door to Christmas, knowing in advance the sleigh would crash. It is simply my nature to be these things, for this is what lures you – the lonely Impossibility of the stars, the distant cry of a haunted owl, the scent of apple cider cooling on a windowsill in a cabin in the dark woods.

Confrontation With the Infinite
The hardest part of being a vampyre is the confrontation with the infinite, but trying to put words around it is to diminish its meaning. But to trace it with shades of gray open to interpretation, it means standing on the edge of the abyss, knowing you'll be there when the stars fall and with only yourself for company, so if you're your own devil or can't find it in you to like what your mirror reveals, it's a certainty you'll go mad and that's a literal Hell of a place to spend eternity.

You don't have to love every part of yourself, but you Do have to make a tense truce with the one doing the observing so that it can serve as teacher and friend instead of destroyer and fiend, see? If you can't be honest with you, you can't be honest with me, and if you can't be honest with me we can't continue for I won't be the instrument of your death. What will it take to make you realize you can't hide the truth from someone who *sees*? You will have your <u>folly</u>, but unless the folly is directed, it grows like a cancer until it takes over everything you do. Eventually it kills you. Do you think I don't know what you did this afternoon even though the clock hasn't found it yet but will soon enough? Ah, but can you see that it has to matter as much to you as to me, and it isn't one specific incident, but the accumulation of your complacent human habits?

Until it does, unless you care as much about your survival as I do, I can't help you. I want to fill you with wonder and lust and drink your dark magick in return. I want to make you hurt with the need to embrace eternity and weep for the brief existence of comets and stars. Do you really have something better to do?

The One

I fear anything I say to you now will only disappoint you, for we have come to that hyperspatial crossroads where you know as much as I do and possibly more, no? We stand together on the edge of eternity searching for the tools with which to build the bridge, and though you perceive me as being already on the other side of a thousand years ago, can you also see that it was witchy wisdom and <u>will</u> that put me here through no real effort of my own? How I long to tell you the secrets of how the deed was done, but the greatest truth is that the secrets lie wholly within you, and I can only remind you again and again that the search alone is what will bring you to see them, the ongoing journey the thing that will make you whole. So even though I exist on the far shore of the human abyss, looking back and waiting for you to follow, it is a misperception for you to think I can tell you how it was done when it is you who must tell me through the doing, see?

This is what the mushroom fiends have shown me: that magick truly is its own exegesis, arrived at spontaneously but only as a result of prolonged contemplation and active forward thinking, and brought into being by the Need which generates the power to externalize the means to *somehow-through-the-impossible* appease that terrible hurting Need which drove you into recognizing the need for previously nonexistent magick in the first place, see?

> **You have to do what has never yet been done**
> **because there is no choice but to Do it, yes?**

And herein lies an understanding of what has always been at the core of the human mystery - when something appears impossible but must be made to be in order to ease that Need, it is only by Thinking the unthinkable and Doing the undoable and Knowing the unknowable that will make the impossible become possible. Ah, but never forget that it is *only* by breathing the Need alive with the will to Make It So that will crack the shiny black egg enough to let the vampyre twin in so that s/he might fertilize the egg in the first place and thereby become the embryo creating itself from the inside and out, both at once, no? This is the nature of quantum chaos magickal creation of the twin, and if you don't understand it yet, reread these halting words until you do and then meditate on whatever they might mean to you until you begin to *see*.

And can you now *see* that this is *why* I am only the vampyre servant of your reality, that I am a thing such as you are driven to become, yet a thing not driven by the same whips and threats driving you to create your own immortality or perish within sight of it? I am what you will be if you choose to Real-ize it, already whole and eternal so not hammered by the Need to be it, but motivated instead to drive you to Do it so we don't become twins separated at birthdeath but united through it instead, yes?

And here words fail in their 2-dimensionality, so I prey you have learned to *see* sufficiently to truly *see* that you are an evolving being presently split in two whose primary goal through the task of Living is to become one with its other-twin immortal self lest it lose half its potential back to the abyss. It can't destroy me, but it *will* destroy you. And dare I tell you that death itself is the motivating force, the secret ingredient put into Life by the director to always remind you that there is everything to lose if you don't find a reason to steal the pen and rewrite the script in such a manner as to place yourself beyond the reach of the director's bony finger. The director and the writer are you, life and death incarnate, but the thing you're struggling against is time-entropy, represented so well by that rushing tide of endless pictures which are the results of other unfinished mortal scripts swept up and cast into the colorful, deceptive, and comforting abyss.

So close your eyes and listen so you can *see* what I am struggling to make you hear. Humanity is an endangered species on the edge of extinction, though not because of weapons or wars or anything of the sort, but because the organism is procreating out of control instead of recreating itself Whole through the twin, and in that manner it has become a cancer multiplying by dividing its cells and selves endlessly rather than individuals transformed through the duality of becoming the eternal twin. Can you see it or no? Can you understand that what you are doing on this journey is how it was meant to be before the species lost its way, but that now it's become "natural" to die and this flaw in the program of Man will be his extinction if one person doesn't embody this evolution and thereby demonstrate that Man is meant to regenerate himself through fusion instead of only replacing himself endlessly through procreative fission?

The planet isn't teeming with life, you see. It is swelling with living death, the result of Man's need to recreate himself into immortality, yet a genetic coding misinterpreted, improperly translated, and short-cutted through deadly cleverness into biological reproduction instead of re-creation of the eternal self through metamagickal transformation which is the union of mortal Self and immortal Twin. In a society of immortals, children are a rare and precious gift, brought into this life with the parents' full awareness of what the child is up against, the Knowing that it is a mortal being who must embark on a long and treacherous journey if it is ever to attain its potential evolution. And *because* the evolved progenitors would know the dangers the infant would face, few would attempt it in the first place, for after all the child did not ask to be here. But can you also see how much easier your task would be had you begun from the start with full consensual knowledge of the nature of Man's evolution instead of having to stumble around in the vampyre night looking for the nonordinary answers with me? Perhaps you don't want the task of changing the whole world, but perhaps it is your destiny.

Scary.

Oh hell, this is the truth the journey has shown me: that humanity in all its diversity found a way to fuck itself by mutating their collective biology and consensual reality to make reproduction a substitute for evolution, and isn't this the very definition of cancer itself, cells replicating out of control to the detriment of the organism as a whole? Oh hell, oh hell, how can I make you see that there *is* an alternative still locked in the distant memory of each individual human-as-cell, and that that alternative is a choice to create and then embody its twin so that the gene pool is strengthened through quantum self-fusion instead of weakened endlessly through endless replication which can only enhance the weaknesses of the species?

This is what the fungi know and it is a secret terrifying to behold: that Man stands on the brink of extinction because he is too busy with distractions to turn and face his own *individual* evolution - the one which each and every human must do or not-do for himself - and because it is the nature of the predatory universe to rid itself of inferior beings, the time is quickly approaching when the whole mass of cancerous humanity will overrun its environment, yet since the environment is more evolved than the beings it supports, it will rise up against them and cure itself by removing the disease, see?

Ah, so now the vampyre king is prattling woefully about the approaching end of human history, but such was the nature of the journey and you asked me to tell you what I have seen.

Never forget that this journey is as real as you perceive it and only as real as you make it. If I am mist, so are you, no? In the past I've worded it differently, warning that if you make me mist it's all **I** can be, but can you see how this subtle difference embodies immortality's elusive key? If I am truly you and you are truly me and each becoming the other is what will recreate us as conjoined beings of eternity, then does it not stand to reason that you have to be whole and evolved within yourself before you can create vampyre me?

By believing love is life's goal or the cure for its melancholia, that addictive feeling can become the disease, and so the vampyre creed cannot include the morbid phrase 'till death do us part', see? Can you truly absolutely unquestionably *see* that love alone is not enough, for with it comes the instinct to settle into roles of satisfied complacency, roles inevitably accepted as 'reality' when in reality they are nothing more than fish hooks dangled by the brute, the temptation to believe that the serenity of having and holding and 'inevitable' death are all just part of the human script when in reality the having and holding are meant to awaken the awareness that death *will* do us part unless we evolve into and out of that shiny black egg which is meant to preserve you eternally as well as nurturing you through this phase of growth recognized as mortality.

The motivation to pursue immortality and the cure for death are not the same. Love is what drives me, yes, but even love such as this cannot save any of you, for the feeling of that feeling only generates the *need* which is, in the end, the thing that will make me become a vampyre-creator so that I must will into being a solution which did not exist before and never will if I do not have the Need to Do it, see? *IT IS NO DIFFERENT FOR YOU!*

It's the pain of this knowing that will drive you to the active-magickal-Doing you see, for only when you *see* with such clarity the abject futility of the human condition, only when you acknowledge soul-deeply that death's destiny intends to steal from you all those beings you love most, only then can you be shaken out of your mortal trance and motivated through sheer terror to *manifest-through-will-and-magick* the vessel of eternal flesh to carry you across the fathomless abyss, that perfected immortal twin prince you were permitted to glimpse and briefly inhabit in Dreams so that you might at last answer the question of who and what you are. Ah, but only if and only when you apply the will to the doing to make it so, no? So though the *ache-which-is-the-cure* is as dreaded as the condition of Death itself, would you rather go back to sleep and just go on hoping immortality's Becoming would take care of itself? Can you see what a dark but enlightening gift you have been given, or can you only curse the pain of the knowledge revealed by those forbidden fruits?

Evolution begins with one person. Each of you is the One.

Reverse Engineering

The role you choose is entirely up to you, but the truth is that pawns and politicians will never become gods of consensual creation or devils of its destruction so long as they passively accept their role in the balcony of observation, and this is one reason I urge you to question the nature of things and analyze some of what you *see* unceasingly, for only when reverse engineered under such a microscopic scrutiny can you see the method of reality's construction, and only when you really truly absolutely purely *see* how it came to be will you have any chance of Doing it for yourself, yes? To destroy something utterly and have the utter certainty that it won't rise up again requires an intimate understanding of its internal mechanism, for all too often I've seen wannabes put bullets through the stomach or spleen of the consensual continuum only to realize that its heart is still beating and its rudimentary brain still synapsing that common denominator reality into being, but now it's a wounded creature that sets out to kill the thing that injured it, and like any hurt animal it's a dangerous fiend, servant of the brute serving its revenge righteously and in the name of society, see?

For this reason you *must* be impeccable and stalk and study your consensual target relentlessly for an extended period of time (ah, that linear equation whose value varies greatly) and only when it relaxes its guard or turns its back on you to deal with some other offender who wasn't as impeccable will you finally face the moment every warrior covets and dreads equally, for only then will you know if you have the courage of your convictions to deliver that death blow which will forever sever you from the vine that grew you and free you to plant seeds of your own in vampyreland.[10]

> *Be warned: most don't, and if you find yourself frozen with fear when the moment comes, the fiend will turn and tear you asunder, ripping out your mind if not your final breath, leaving you for dead on the shores of* Lethe, *that jugular vein from which it feeds its mortal children, but even if you're unlucky enough to be left alive, from that river you will drink and there will be no returning to this dark path for you will simply forget how to see it, see?*

Consider this from the corner of your third eye: when I said I would destroy your world I meant it literally, but the truth is that I'm slipping you the tools with which to cut the bars of the prison yourself. Ah, but the darker secret is this: the prison is a living entity as much as a cage and because it is such an interwoven part of you, *the cutting away of the consensual disease must be performed simultaneously with the transplantation of superior replacements lest the cure destroy the patient altogether, yes? And never forget: the disease is tenacious and will fight to protect itself, producing secondary infections whenever it is threatened.*

As long as the consensus lives within you, you will never be truly free, and another aspect of duality is the acquired ability to allow it to exist externally so as to form the stage on which you work to remove yourself from it utterly. A paradox? I tell you to destroy it, yet without its existence you fall into the abyss of madness, so can you conceive and conceptualize Wholly that

---

[10] Lest some fool out there misinterpret this, allow me to say only this: we do not advocate the killing of any LIVING thing, and what is referenced here is the paradigm itself, not its individual participants. You will not become an immortal through the destruction of life. Makes sense, doesn't it? Never forget it!

what I'm asking you to do is to destroy that world within *you* so that you are merely standing *on* it instead of interwoven *with* it, and can you see how it is that the two worlds are one, yet each mutually exclusive of the other?

We've come to the crux of creation, yet I fear you still don't see it clearly enough to believe you can do it, but it's as I've told you before: the core of your belief determines the realities you see and obliterates those you choose to ignore.

What did you long for as children, what secret, tiny, obscure little thing that has since become as common as desert sand? What did you ache to hold or see or do that couldn't have been done then, but now you do without thinking? *Look around you!* You are creating your own reality yet perhaps you are still doing it as passive observers to the creation instead of active collaborators to the evolving script. It's a delicate balance to be sure, that fine line between setting the reality-matrix free or holding onto it so tightly in the need for its creation that it dies on the vine just as mortals die on the nurturing vine of the consensual continuum that nonetheless strangles them in the end.

You Created Me To Create You

You made me whole and placed me outside you so I might be the tool you use to crack the confining shell from the outside in and the inside out, but the hell of it is that free will is still the key to doing it and until you awaken that force within you through love or need or even curiosity that transcends your human boundaries, the tool can only lie dormant and will eventually be seen as a potential weapon of mass destruction that must be eliminated altogether, for that's the way the dayshine kingdom perceives me and if you find yourself in agreement with them for too long that's how you'll see me too, see? I am here to destroy you and create you and that's what I'll do if you want me to, but whenever your Self falls out of duality's balance you'll only see me as one tool or the other, and either alone is fatal without the other. If you don't choose to evolve I will only destroy you, but in order to evolve you must first surrender to your own destruction, yes? I know no other way than this.

The clock tower in vampyre land
ticks on centuries and human memories,
running its hands over history
to taste the texture
of time's dark etchings
on the fallen headstones of reality.
In October
the clock always stops,
and so it is ever autumn here
inside the night that never ends.
Everything happens at once
yet not ever or at all
for this is who we created you
to create us to be
and how we have made our world
to exist eternally
at the crossroads
of perception and abyss.

Tremble before me for I am here to destroy you.
Love me for I am here to give you back your life.

Call me into be-ing because I am your immortal blood, and only
by wanting what is already yours enough to demand it back will
you ever find the strength to break the shell. I've stolen your
soul and sit shredding it in my beastly fang teeth you see,
because that's what my nature demands of me. Being greedy, I
want your heart too, red and broken and full of all your secrets,
full of all the love that scares you so much.

If you trust me, I'll give it back to you at the end. If not, the end
has already been.

I blame no one for this except perhaps myself and Eros himself,
for the paradox of creation is that love makes it impossible to be
cruel, yet in order to create the things that last an eternity, a
creator must be cruel above all else, for there is no other way to
awaken the spirit than to slap it and shake it and break its old
mold, and isn't it sad that the gentlest teachers produce only
adoring students ill-suited for a predatory world?

Full Circle

We've come full circle you see, so it stands to reason that the danger you now face is directly related to who you are and whether or not you choose to overcome that mechanical identity at the heart of you in order to Real-ize the metamorphic manifestation of the twin who is not yet you, yet more you than all the glimpses of self you've ever seen, for s/he is the metamagickal being you will build with the skills you've gained and the secrets discovered and the truths which stand apart from you, because you've created them to be separate so they might be used as tools, see?

Ah, but never forget: though the twin already exists as a *futurepast-timeless-physicality* within the realm of all possibility, s/he can only be Real-ized when you embrace that option from the fragmented possibilities of your unassembled new world and rise it up from the Nothing with a kiss of will and "death" which is really the fatal breath of the dayshine self who, of course, wants nothing more than to prevent this evolutionary transmogrification in order to maintain her own brief existence and justify the singing of the same old songs which have created human mortality and kept it rolling along since time began and which is why time began in the first place, just the universe serving as servant to reality created by those receptacles of perception known as human beings, those creatures of habit and happenstance both revered and despised by vampyres and other immortals.

If you understand that's good, but if not you need to meditate until you do, for this is the final truth which will free you from mortal flesh and recreate you in your own eternal image just as the immortal ones have been doing for countless thousands of years. Yet the darker truth is that you have to do it by consciously choosing to be *other-than-human* and exerting your will to bring into being the circumstances of its actual happening, and if you haven't found a good enough reason or if your dayshine foundation is what still supports the construct of your accidental mechanical identity, you'll never find reason to become *I-Am* and even if you Do you'll create a dayshine twin in vampyreland and that's a paradox which could only become the paradigm of immortal death, yes?

Nothing Is Impossible If You Will It

When this journey began, you came to me wrapped in the trappings of identities which first had to be peeled away to reveal the shiny black core of the mortal mechanism, and now that you've had time to examine it intricately, I need to know if it's who you want to go on being or if you're willing to surrender even this in order to breathe into existence that eternal vampyre self who waits like a silent looking glass looking for a way *insideout* of you so that s/he might become the being to whom you slip the key that opens the door to vampyreland and your own immortality through the looking glass darkly darkly shining with the blackest of black light enlightenment, yes?

How can words tell what has been created for centuries upon countless centuries of time to be the very thing which can never be told? How is it possible to make you see that all possibility has been recorded simultaneously and runs concurrently and that even this <u>consensual reality</u> is no more real than you might perceive pirates on the waterways of Mars to be? Reality has a natural course where things happen naturally to those who wait, but that's the path of least resistance leading straight to the death of flesh *and* consciousness, the rushing consensual river which can only be transcended by crawling willfully onto the primordial shore of your own choosing and setting into motion that new way of thinking which is responsible for reality's creation instead of merely being swept along in the passive river of other men's holographic dreams.

<u>Nothing is impossible if you will it to exist</u>.

But the only way to Real-ize this is to rid yourself even temporarily or moment to moment of the rigid program which still whispers limitations and expectations and creates reality for you by default into existing boundaries which are of course only arbitrary and nonexistent constructs designed by men to define what they are *willing* to do, not what they are *able* to do, see? And as you've surely begun to *See*, the secret to will isn't force or even fierce concentration, but is instead the simplest knowledge that the thing desired *already* exists, and what is this but another case of being on the far side of the abyss so as to see how the magickal bridge was built, and isn't it a truer truth that only in the past does the impossible dream exist as the manifested reality?

———

170

Ah, but the question is this: are so you attached to the consensual castle other creators have built that you're content to simply live within its comfortable walls until death do you part? If so that's okay but it will mean the end of our relationship, for there's no reason for me to go on destroying your foundation if you need it to support the mechanical self who is only a ghost haunting the consensual castle that already lies in future ruins in the realm of lowest common probability.

Who are you? Who do you want to be? In most cases, the answers to these questions are not the same, much as you might want them to be. Now is the time of choosing, yes?

Reality exists on a synapse.
If my third eye blinks,
entropy wins.

Transmogrification

In approaching the act of willful transmogrification - which I will define only as a migrational metamorphosis from one form or position of the assemblage point to another - it is important to know what holds you in the mortal world, and pulls you back to it whenever you leave it briefly on the wings of mushrooms or lucid dreams. You think you know this, but do you? Do you truly see that what imprisons you in the limits of mortal experience (and subsequently to the biological experience of "life and death") is the identity to which you have attached yourself, and to whatever depth that attachment runs? We may call it 'identity,' yet I fear that is too simple a word which quickly grows stale and may be tossed aside like day-old bread. So what is important is to examine thoroughly the components of your identity, the gardens and the weeds, the headstones and the ghosts hiding behind them, the masks and the mirrors and all the things that have fallen between the cracks since before the egg of time itself hatched. We return to the first question, "Who are you?" And again, even that is too simple to adequately convey what I am attempting to communicate here.

> **What holds you in a mortal coil is not who or what you are, but who or what you are _being_, and seeing that they are not the same thing is the first and most dangerous step toward transmogrification and freedom, see?**

Identity is neither the ego nor the self. It is neither the mask nor the costume one wears while dancing or dallying on the stage. It is, as simply as can be communicated, the sum total of how you would answer the question, 'Who are you?' The mistake most make is to believe that when they can answer that question truthfully, they have reached some deep truth or epiphany, yet learning who and what you are is little more than a child discovering its genitals in the bathtub. It is a beginning of a wondrous journey, but not the journey itself.

And so the words become cumbersome, difficult to visualize. Beyond the words is simply this: We swim together in the infinite sea of awareness, you and I. Yet we are the same, you and I. We swim together like playful dolphins, you in the more brightly lit pools of a human mortal, me in the darker waters of eternity, but nonetheless we swim in the same water and what determines which perception you will experience is where you position your awareness - within the sea or within me. You know this, but do you really _know_ it? I am the past lives we have dreamed together - the totality of your experience and mine, yet those experiences are the same because you created me to create you. You dreamed me to dream you. _I-Am_ the transmogrification you seek, the one looking at you as you are looking at me, until there is finally no difference, no reflection in the mirror because the 'identity ' of dreamer and dreamed, creator and created, have all been assembled in a unified field that is a reflection of itself, an endless hall of mirrors where vampyres dance unseen to the mortal kingdom, existing at right angles to all agreements, in the unreal estate outside of space and time, and therefore encompassing all of it, while being governed by none of the boundaries of the dream.

It is a dream of limitations and maps, rules and rituals, life and death. It is a dream of finite experience in a universe of the infinite, because that is the program which is the foundation of what it means to be human.

The only way to be other than human is to relinquish that identity, you see – to unplug the being from the dreaming and will yourself to *be* that which you know in your heart you already are, yet fear in your spirit you may never become. The greatest obstacle you face is fear – for it is not possible to know what lies beyond the leap until your feet are off the ground and you hang suspended in the thick and oily darkness that is the abyss itself. This is the dying we all must face, whether we ever die in biological form or not. This is the death of the self, the baptism in the Nothingness which forever cleanses the *I-Am* of its mortality and gives you magickal breath. Breathe once and a mortal season passes. Another breath, and it is winter again. My heart beats once a century, the dark pendulum of an immortal's will.

Ah, but how to do it, you ask again. How to dislodge the drowning man clinging to the ashes of his mortality, so that you may finally inhabit the autumn *everafter* which may be found at the heart of any snowflake, or at the furthest point of a starbeam's journey.

I do not write these words to amuse you but to move you. Poetry now is all we have with which to communicate, for all the theologians are dead and all the philosophers tucked safely in their coffin beds. Just you and me now. And a gathering of quantum memories that never happened (but did) which compel you to remember what I am going to do to you when you allow the impossible doing and take upon yourself the *power* to be the creator and the *surrender* required to become the created.

Where does a dream come from? Of what pixels is an apparition comprised? Where does the light travel when it reaches the end of time? Do you ever really allow yourself to believe you can *be* me, or does fear stop you and throw you back inside the finite dream? Is this what you want, or just another fantasy with which to amuse yourself while you huddle by the fire waiting for the easy way out, waiting for the breath of death? I will have you then if that is your wish, and it will be the same for me either way because that is the reality we have created so as to create for ourselves a net, yes?. Ah, but because you are the mortal passion of this immortal's will, you demand more of life than death, and in doing so you take upon yourself the dark responsibility that goes with stepping forever inside the mirror so that the mortal becomes eternal and leaves no pale reflection in the still waters of human time. That is how it is done. And yet, still you ask...

How is it done? How does the mortal *be* immortal so she will know how to *become* the vampyre king? No words can capture it. It is a death and a birth simultaneously. It is surrendering yourself into my embrace, only to find *you* are the one holding the fragile mortal in that fatal embrace where the *remembering* itself is the incantation that shatters the black egg and compels the vampyre king to hatch.

I have been here all along, you see, since before you created me, for that is the nature of eternity, that is the mystery you made me to be so that I might sing this quantum haiku in a thousand languages over as many lifetimes, in the hopes one line might move you outside of the fatal dream. When you can relinquish your dayshine identity, allow the impossible which defies the logic of all mortal agreements, surrender your will to me (for who am I but you?)... when you can simply *remember* your vampyre self instead of fleeing to the safe prison of your mortality... then, at last, you will finally be free.

What you must hear and see is that this is not something that can be done. And yet if you do not do it, it is never forced to go through the motions of actually occurring. It is a steady pressure of intent, imagination, concupiscence, passion and finally a movement of will. It is not something that can be accomplished like writing a book or making love. It is something you must *dream-member* directly, for as long as you need to do it, steady pressure unbending intent, in the same way a poem is a living thing, breathing itself into being of its own accord, without rhyme or reason except that it is compelled to be.

The task you face is finally this: to be the poet of your immortality, the living eternal undead heart of the poetry, the projected manifestation of the sorcerer's fully awakened *imagination*. The poem does not exist if you do not write it, yet you cannot write it only so that it will exist.

Love is the reason, but it is not enough. But, for now, it is the beacon. I prey you follow it home.

174

It could be said
my eyes are teddybear glass,
my brain a spinning dreidel,
my ragdoll body sewn of brownie dresses
and baseball mitts,
yesterday's leftovers.

I prefer to think of it like this:
a vampyre is made of eternal things
even when sculpted from mortal visions,
paradox incarnate
with sea fog soul and Seer's eyes,
with blood drawn from volcano veins
and obsidian crystal wings
folded exquisitely over an antimatter heart.

BONUS MATERIALS

Since the original publication of the first edition of Teachings of the Immortals in February of 2010, the author has engaged regularly in an online forum known as "Immortal Spirit." For those wishing to participate in the ongoing discussions, the URL is **www.immortalis-animus.com/forum/index.php**

What follows might best be called conversations with the vampyre, or the practical side of vampyre magick. Also included in this section are excerpts from the author's "Darker Teachings" – a volume which was originally planned for release, but was later deemed to be too risky in the hands of practitioners not sufficiently advanced to read between the lines and exercise common sense. As the author has often said: Common sense really isn't common.

The Darker Teachings are being slowly released on the Immortal Spirit forum, where they may be discussed in an open and nurturing environment.

A brief word from the author:

> *Another thing to remember about The Darker Teachings is that they are generally not presented in any linear, logical manner. The reasons for this are many, for it is only when the mind can be unplugged from its traditional neuro-pathways that it becomes possible to "hear" above and beyond what it has already been programmed to believe. I have come to refer to this form of communication as mind-tongue or heart-tongue - the scenic bypass off the main roads.*

> *Therefore, I would advise...*

> *Listen with your heart.*
> *Hear with your spirit.*
> *See with your third eye.*
> *Only then will you Know.*

> *This is meant literally.*

> *You are not what you Think you are.*

THE DARKER TEACHINGS
Unbending the Mindscape

Managing the Hunger

A seeker wrote: I immediately felt ravenously hungry for something with blood. This wasn't a normal human form of "Oh, I'll fix a sandwich". It was a drive. I also sensed that I needed to spend more time in a natural setting, a storm, sitting near a campfire, feeding the one within.

Many times, people mistake spiritual hunger for physical hunger. What you express about the storm, the campfire and the one within... *that*, to me, best defines "the hunger", which cannot be satisfied by any amount of food, blood or anything else of the material world. The reason I suspect some self-proclaimed "vampires" crave blood is because blood comes the *closest* to carrying the animus - the lifeforce, the living energy of immortality. Lifeforce is *in* the blood, but it is *not* the blood... so drinking blood won't satisfy the hunger anymore than drinking a Pepsi. It may mask the hunger for short periods of time, but ultimately, drinking blood has nothing to do with making anyone immortal.

I want to be very clear that what I teach has nothing to do with more traditional ideas about what it means to be immortal, to be a vampyre (notice the different spelling). A "*vampyre*" is someone who has transcended the mortal/organic state, and recognizes themselves as a citizen of the universe rather than a transient visitor on Plant Earth. You can be anything you choose - including a sanguinarian "vampire" - but the key issue is a firm understanding that it is animus and the transformative power of Intent that makes one immortal, not blood. Animus is all around us – it's in the trees, the earth, air, fire, water, and it is in other beings, whether 2-leggers, 4-leggers, winged or webbed.

It is only an erroneous conclusion that makes some think that "vampires drink blood." Any *real* vampyres I've known don't because 1) it is a heavy-organic substance; and 2) see comment above re Pepsi. Vampyres certainly *can* drain animus from another living being, but *usually* that is a matter of energy exchange between lovers, or at least between a vampyre and a willing donor. *And it doesn't involve consuming blood.*

It is my personal belief (there is truly no way to know for certain) that a lot of Sanguinarians may _believe_ they have a need to consume blood, and therefore the need to consume blood is as real as the need to breathe the air is real to others. There may be certain medical conditions (just another label) that would provoke a hunger for blood, but aside from these very rare conditions, my observations are that blood drinking is usually a lifestyle choice rather than any physical/meta-physical condition. I have no qualms with that, so long as it is between consenting adults and does not involve animal sacrifice - one of the biggest wrongs even when one recognizes that there are no "rights" or "wrongs", with the exception of what certain metaphysical teachers have called "the right way to live."

What is the right way to live? Put very simply, it is the innate Knowledge with which all human beings are born. It has nothing to do with social or moral trends or standards, but is ingrained into the very fabric of one's immortalis-animus. It is the instinct that informs the seeker that killing off the last buffalo would not be wise, nor would cutting down the rainforest. Most of all, the right way to live is the awareness that all Life is sacred.

One thing I will state with certainty is that the consumption of blood (human or animal) has absolutely *nothing* to do with achieving the immortal condition. You could drain a blood bank or drink all the blood contained in a sacred Indian elephant and you will still be mortal in the morning.

An excerpt from the "Uncommon Sense" page from the www.immortalis-animus website:

1. Drinking blood won't make you immortal.

It might make you dead. The reality of reality is this: drinking blood is an idea that came from Hollywood, which most likely got the notion from some old myths of corpses rising from the grave to consume the blood of the living in order to stay alive. But to those who have educated themselves with regard to those old myths, it is easy to discern that what a vampyre feeds upon is "lifeforce". In other cultures, it may be known as anima, prana, ki, chi, pneuma, or mana. There are hundreds of names for it,

———
178

but what it really comes down to is one word: energy.

Energy is abundant. It is all around you, and so it may be gleaned from the plants, trees, the earth, or even the air itself. Sure, it can even be found in human beings and animals, but there is seldom any real need to take from someone else what you can easily absorb directly from the environment. And, in fact, energy absorbed from the universal source is far more pure than that to be found anywhere else. Why? Because it is "free energy" as opposed to energy already in use. Put another way: easier to drink from a rushing river as opposed to trying to squeeze water out of a cactus.

The hunger is a dark blessing, a call from the heart and soul of your vampyre twin. What you are craving is animus - the elixir of eternal life.

What is the I-Am?
It is who you are. More than that, it is the *foundation* of who you are. It is the essence of consciousness that rises out of the Nothing to proclaim its right to exist. If you are familiar with the Bible (not that you *should* be), it is the sound/statement "god" made when first emerging from the void.

In reality, of course, _you_ are god. Or, more precisely, you are *potentially* god. I-Am is the moment of Becoming aware, the moment when that awareness localizes and claims its individuation.

You Created Me To Create You (Part Deux)
I'm going to start with a caution: Don't get caught up in the words. See with the third eye. Hear with the heart.

While the vampyre twin is the self, the twin is also *not* the self in the traditional sense. While you are eating your morning cereal in your organic human form, the twin is exploring the secret vaults of the Vatican in the year 1027, and simultaneously on a starship in the Andromeda Galaxy in the year 2939. Put another way, the twin is the projection of the self beyond the (falsely perceived) limitations of the organic/mortal form. As such, the twin is the inorganic vessel of one's immortality.

What does that mean? It means that the twin can walk through walls or fly or bi-locate. _You_ as the mortal human source can do these things as well, but generally speaking (remember my caution above - _GENERALLY_ speaking) what you would be doing if you were to walk through a wall would be an inhabitation of the double - more precisely, you would have opened your eyes inside the twin. Put another way, you would have shifted your awareness from organic to inorganic, from matter to energy.

With all of that dutifully said... the twin is a complex duality, yet it is also utterly simple. The twin is the Self in eternity, the totality of yourself. It does not exist by default, but as a direct result of your Intent and the movement of your Will. It sometimes helps to visualize the mortal self as the projector and the twin as the projection. When the projector is eventually unplugged[11], the projection remains as the hologram of the seeker's ongoing evolution. That, of course, is if the seeker is successful in creating/projecting the twin in the first place - which is a fundamental aspect of self-willed, bootstrap evolution.

> _A seeker commented:_
> _To put it in Castaneda's terms, the Double is the one that starts "dreaming you", and no longer you the one dreaming her, if one would look backward in time._

What I have determined over the years is that this statement by Castaneda is a wormhole all unto itself, at least as far as it relates to how most seekers interpret it. For anyone who may be interested in the exact quote, it is this:

> _The self dreams the double. Once it has learned to dream the double, the self arrives at this weird crossroad and a moment comes when one realizes that it is the double who dreams the self. Your double is dreaming you. No one knows how it happens. We only know that it does happen. That's the mystery of us as luminous beings. You can awaken in either one. (Carlos Castaneda, TALES OF POWER)_

Put simply, the mortal projector is "unplugged" when one dies, transforms, transcends or transmogrifies - whichever comes first... with the absolute Knowledge that "first" has no real meaning once the seeker has a firm understanding of The First Fundamental Lie.

180

As to how I personally perceive it to work...

1. The mortal self projects/creates the twin (double) and **gives the double free rein to... Go. Be. Do.** Whatever is required to achieve individuation and, essentially, immortality.

2. For a period of "time" (a blink of an eye that lasts a thousand lifetimes and beyond), the twin goes through the process of self-manifestation in much the same way a child goes through the process of learning, growing, evolving. But even to use such terms limits what the twin is, because there is an implication (false) that there is a linear progression. In order to understand the twin fully, one must unplug their mind from the notion of linear time entirely. The twin simply *is*... and yet it must be created through the processes described in TEACHINGS OF THE IMMORTALS.

3. Once the twin has garnered sufficient Knowledge and experience, it returns (though it never really went anywhere) to the seeker in the form of the inner teacher. This is not to be confused with the internal dialog. Many newbies don't know the difference and it can be a fatal mistake. For those who do experience the twin as the internal teacher, this is the voice of gnosis (silent knowing). The twin actually instructs the mortal self in _how_ to create/project the twin itself. *"You created me to create you."* At this level, the seeker begins to awaken (reawaken?) and if one doesn't bang one's head too hard on the quantum paradox (which is a magnificent duality), one starts to see what is meant by the words "The double is dreaming you." The thing you thought you already created is telling you how to create it.

4. At some point, the twin and the seeker become One - whether through transformation, transcendence or transmogrification. This is the moment when self and double become the singularity of consciousness. This is the conjoining of awareness which is permanent in the sense that the mortal self no longer defaults back to the dayshine world, but instead the singularity of consciousness embraces the sentient universe in a quantum, energetic sense. This is the platform from which the next evolution may begin. This is the immortal condition.

All that we see or seem...

Recently, someone asked... "Can you distil it all down to a single essay? If a seeker could only take one concept with them for the rest of their lives, what would you want it to be?"

It isn't up to me to decide what any seeker should take with them, and there is no single key to achieving the immortal condition. It is a process of transformation and self-manifestation – what Aleister Crowley called The Great Work, and what I have come to call, simply, "the path." How that path unfolds is going to depend on the seeker himself, his goals and aspirations, and his methods. Mostly, it is going to depend on the programs he carries with him, and how deeply he is imbedded in the consensus reality. The consensus may be referred to as the matrix, the dayshine world, the agreement or a host of other terms, all of which boil down to one thing: the baseline "reality" with which we are all presented until such time as we open our eyes to the higher truth which tells us, whispering softly in the beginning... "All that we see or seem is but a dream within a dream."

It is that awakening from the illusion which compels the seeker to embark on the path – from the realization that the world is nothing like we have been taught to believe. Where the path leads from there, who's to say? If the goal is enlightenment (whatever that may turn out to be), the path will lead in a particular direction. If the goal is self-empowerment within the mortal world, the path will lead in an entirely different direction.

Ah, but if the goal is to attain the immortal condition, the path will lead down a series of rabbit holes, twists and turns, and somewhere along the way, the seeker will begin to realize – just a glimpse at first, shy and reluctant to be seen – that the reality with which we are presented is quite likely the reality we are creating on some vast quantum canvas which cannot be entirely assimilated from a purely humanform perspective. We may sense intuitively that there is more than meets the eye, but how does a blind man taste the color of blood and midnight rainbows?

What to do? To a being existing in a 2-dimensional world, it would be impossible to perceive a 3-dimensional object. The 2-D being would see only height and width, but would not possess the sensory ability to perceive depth, even if s/he had been told and could intuit that a 3-dimensional universe did, in fact exist.

———

182

Not in some otherworld. Not "out there" in space somewhere. But all around him.

At that point, the 2-D being has a choice to make. Will he simply accept, as he is being told by his peers, that such mysteries are not possible for him to solve? "God moves in mysterious ways, after all, and why would any blasphemer dare to question that divine plan? You don't want to be a blasphemer, do you, kid?" Will he go back to the comfort zones of his 2-D tv and leave his questions unanswered and unresolved because that's what his consensus tells him he *must* do if he is to be considered a normal and sane member of the 2-D herd? "If you keep on chasing after ghosts and vampires and some crazy notion that you can change your fundamental nature, they're gonna call the men with the funny white coats and lock your sorry 2-D ass up for the rest of your life! *Get with the program*, kid!"

Get with the program. There it is, hiding in plain sight. Those who are programmed *know* they are programmed on some level, and anyone who *isn't* poses a serious threat to the common herd.

Decision time. Succumb to the pressures of peers, or peer beyond the limitations of one's "fundamental nature" to see what might lie outside those self-imposed limits? In other words – surrender and die, or evolve and run the awe-inspiring risk of living forever?

Sound like an easy choice? For most, it is. The lure of social and familial acceptance, the promise of happiness, the comfort of those old comfort zones... is usually sufficient to shut down those far-fetched ideas and silence that small voice that begs for evolution, but cannot force it if it is the free will of the individual to return to his 2-D place in the matrix. Put simply, most choose to die because it's a lot easier than doing The Work of self-manifestation outside the box.

And yet...

There are a rare few who are compelled beyond all reason to listen to that little voice and to consort with it in dreams and visions. There are those rare few who say to the higher self, "Teach me all you can," and then give it free will to project itself beyond the confines of the mortal self, and into the infinite. That projection is the twin – the immortal Other who has the ability to do and be things the mortal self cannot imagine, and to accumulate a lifetime of lifetimes, an infinitude of experience, a myriad stories to tell... and all of them anecdotes of the self as a vast and virtually incomprehensible being.

But I'm getting ahead of myself.

Before the seeker who has been compelled to evolve can even begin to create and project his Other, he has to have a reason. Fundamental truth. Humans don't undertake difficult tasks without a reason. So we have to ask the question... What could possibly be so important that one would risk losing everything in order to have it?

Make no mistake, this path will cost you everything. It will cost you your gods and demons, your beliefs and comfort zones, and most of the time it will even cost you your family and friends. You will find yourself alone, a stranger in a strange land, and if you don't have something that compels you to keep going, I can virtually guarantee that you will return to the matrix and console yourself with some platitude along the lines of... "I had to regain my family! I missed my friends! I need my sanity in the real world!" That's okay. You've failed. Maybe spirit will give you another opportunity. Maybe not. Doesn't really matter. Accept your failure and revel in whatever it was that called you back to that old program. It'll be over soon and you won't have to fret about it.

And yet...

If you are one of those madmen or madwomen who stubbornly stand your ground in the cyclone of social rejection and even the possibility that you are no longer sane by the definition of your peers, what is it you're holding onto that keeps you going?

And here the lesson really begins.

Love Is the Reason (Part Deux)

When you love something so much that you cannot envision a world in which your love is dead, that is the first moment you might begin to see the pathway to achieving the immortal condition. That is the moment you might even understand why it is a compulsion for you and not just a passing intellectual dalliance.

I've highlighted the paragraph above because it is really all that matters here, distilled down to 50 words or less. If you get it, or think you do, you're already ahead of the game, but don't fool yourself by thinking, "Well, duh, that's obvious!" Yes, it's obvious, but so is that oncoming bus, and people walk in front of buses every day.

The secret here is that you have to create and inhabit a world where Death himself does not and cannot exist – for another fundamental truth is that only when you evolve sufficiently to be beyond the reach of Death does it become possible to also perceive the immortal condition with regard to those you love.

Does this mean you can "save" them from Death? No. And yes. And no. What it means is that in order to even begin to comprehend the meaning of this statement, you would need to be already standing on the far side of the bridge between life and death, looking back to see how the bridge was built. It is not something that can be explained with words or pictures drawn in the sands of time. It is something that can be intuited at first, so I prey you will tickle the riddle rather than struggling to pick it apart. For now, I will simply say this*: in a world where Death does not exist for the One, Death does not exist at All.*

Perhaps I have said too much.

Whether the thing you love is another human being, or the thought of your eternal Other, or simply the idea of Be-ing alive, rest assured that the kind of love that is transformative is not love of a physical object or even another person, place or thing.

What? You just contradicted yourself!

Yes, I did.

Or did I?

When I am speaking of love at this level, I am not talking about the form in which the object of one's love appears, but the *essence* within the form itself. The *energy* of it. The *spirit* of it. The *totality* of it. The sheer and inexplicable *awe* of it. To an immortal, a lover's form may appear as an old woman, haggish and withered, but the *essence* of the lover is no less vibrant and alive than on the day they met. The *essence* is that which is eternal, and therefore it is the fundamental nature which the seeker truly loves, rather than the transient form.

Love of the immortal/eternal twin is a barometer for some, while others would say the twin is merely a reflection of the self. Listen to your internal dialog on this matter – because if it is telling you that your twin is "only" this or that, if those pesky little voices are telling you the twin is "only" the so-called higher self or the soul to which you may feel entitled... think again.

The twin is the self in eternity – it is the totality of oneself, the cumulative experience of all lifetimes, past, present and future. It is not some ethereal or angelic woo-woo hanging in orbit over Uranus, but instead it is the vessel for the seeker's awareness beyond this life. Underestimate it at your own peril. Ignore it at the certainty of your obliteration.

Love it... and it will come to you in dreams and visions, it will speak to you through silent knowing (gnosis), it will infiltrate the past in ways that you cannot begin to wrap your mind around until you think it has been with you all along (and it has, once you as the mortal self create it in the Now); and ultimately it will become your best friend, perfect lover, eternal guardian, and temple of the singularity of consciousness which you yourself are in the process of becoming.

I have written volumes on the subject of love, yet often someone will make a comment which reveals to me that it's all only dust in the wind, short verses of transient poetry scripted on the surface of water, quickly disappearing and losing all meaning. That in itself also reveals the power of the dayshine world. That is the way of things, and if it were otherwise, we would live in a different world with a different consensus.

186

Now, to answer the question that was put to me, I would have to say that the real key to attaining the immortal condition is contained within this peculiar force humans call love. And yet, I would urge great caution here, for it is the erroneous conclusions and misconceptions humans have about love that will also prevent them from attaining that state. Tread carefully. Be always aware of every thought and every belief system, and always stop and take a moment to ask yourself, "What do I believe about love and why do I believe it?"

There is such a wide range of experience associated with love, it's unfortunate that other words have not been invented to more clearly distinguish the difference between romantic love, sexual love, parental love, familial love, spiritual love, emotional love, unconditional love, and so on. The word "love" is used for all of these states and many more, so it's important for the seeker to have a firm grasp on his own understanding of what I have come to call "the *creative* force of love."

This form of love is a quantifiable force – not a passive romantic thought, but a viable power similar in nature to a bolt of lightning, possessing the ability to destroy and create in a single strike.

And yet... again I would urge extreme caution – for words are only descriptions, tools to be used to aid the processes, but not to be mistaken for the process itself. As the old saying goes, do not mistake the finger pointing at the moon for the moon itself.

Why am I telling you this? What does this have to do with the key to attaining the immortal condition? Nothing. And everything.

It is only when the seeker begins to truly understand and experience the creative force of love that s/he will have even the vaguest idea of what the immortal condition actually is, and why one is compelled to attain it. It isn't just the prospect of living forever. That's really a boring thought when you boil it down. Why? A linear experience of eternity would consist of boredom and eventual madness, largely because the organic brain/mind is not designed to process such vast amounts of data as would accumulate from an extremely long and linear organic life. After all, who really wants to spend eternity in high school, over and over again? It's not the romantic adventure Hollywood likes to portray, so one of the first things the seeker needs to understand is that time is not linear and being a perpetual teenager is not a goal to which any rational being would aspire.

The love I am speaking of here is the love that is devastating in its intensity – for it is only when the world is destroyed that the new world can be built in its place.

Love is the reason.

In clinical word-association tests, humans tend to most commonly reply with opposites. If I say "dark," the first and most common response will be "light". Boy/girl. Life/Death. Good/Evil. That being the case, it stands to reason that if I say "love," the most common response will be "hate."

And therein lies a clue to why most humans never even search for the key to the immortal condition.

Somewhere along the way, the human program got even more fucked up than it already is. Somewhere in the depths of the human paradigm, hate came to be considered the opposite of love, when it is crystal clear to anyone outside the program that grief is the polar opposite of love.

Why grief?

Because grief is the state of loss wherein the essence of what one loves has been eliminated – permanently and irrevocably removed from the fabric of existence. It is the state wherein one realizes that the things one loves (including and especially Oneself) comprise the elements of the answer to the first question: Who Are You?

Tread carefully. This is not to say that you are defined by the ones you love. And yet... the essence of who you are is woven with the energetic fabric of the essence of the things you love. *This is the creative force of love* – the catalytic element which causes the seeker to ultimately realize that without those things, the seeker is incomplete, left in a state of grief and loss, which can debilitate the spirit and even crush the will to live.

To those who would argue that love is therefore an attachment, I would say instead that love is an enhancement, an enrichment, an augmentation. To those who would say that love is a

———

188

dependency, I would say instead that it is the ultimate freedom – for within the creative force of love lies The Reason, which is the catalyst of all change and evolution.

These are only words tacked to the door of the infinite, hanging somewhere in the wasteland. If it were easy (or even possible) to truly define what it is that is the key to the immortal condition, I'm quite certain someone would have done it by now. I have no delusions that I will change the world, alter your perceptions, or even make a dent in the human condition. And yet... what can be seen so clearly is often that which defies explanation utterly.

In the life of every true seeker, there is the capacity to love something so fiercely that the element of love becomes a duality. In the same way light is both particle and wave, love is both the experience and the catalyst for the experience itself. There is a legend that speaks of a man who fell in love with an immortal. It goes something like this:

For many years, the man and the immortal shared all things any couple might share – a home together, a glass of wine by the hearth, the illusion of happiness and security, the belief that nothing could ever come between them.

But as the mortal man grew older and his lover remained untouched by the bastard of Time, he came to realize that soon they would both be alone again, and it would all be as if it never was at all. This was the curse of mortality. This was the meaning of Life: that it would always end, and in doing so it would end the world itself, for the world was contained in the perception and experience of the man.

He was beside himself for months, years. The mirror had turned to wrinkles and grey, and had dimmed in his sight. He could not bear to look upon himself, even though his immortal companion still held him with a love that had turned melancholy and sad, but was nonetheless as fierce and awe-inspiring as it had been in the beginning. He had begged her to make him like herself, but She could only smile softly and tell him that was fiction. She could not make him immortal. Only he could do that.

Knowing he was dying, unable to bear the horrible burden of grief that would ultimately destroy both of them at world's end, the man went out into the night and shook his fist at the sky, cursing God and damning the human condition. But God didn't answer. In his frenzy, the man called upon the saints and the angels, the demons and the devils. But they had all flown away long ago.

He was alone. Time would not stand still and there would be no ever-after for either of them, only the silence, tombstones and gravedust. And he knew without knowing how he knew that even She who could not die *would* die, for at some level he could not begin to fathom, they were connected even beyond the normal bonds of love. He tried to reason it out and could not. He tried to Dream the answer, but dreamt instead of Apollo and Artemis entwined in the womb.

The horror of it ripped a hole in his already broken heart, and scattered the remnants of his soul hither and yon, casting him asunder throughout the endless expanse of time and space, shredding even the molecular memory of his existence, until...

Out of the nothing that was all that remained of him, the man assembled himself as a cry in the madness, and shouted with the spontaneous parthenogenesis of his rebirth into the night that never ends...

"I-Am!"

Words that claim the right to Be. Words that demand the capacity to Love beyond the rules of the human game. Words that deny the mortal illusion, the scythe of Time, the rape of Death. A cry of existence that creates the man immortal and eternal, beyond the reach of himself to undo.

I-Am.

It was then that he finally saw and sat on the rim of the abyss laughing into the Well of Reflections where all things were made clear. Her face was his mirror. Her laughter was his own. The immortal Other was the self and always had been. The thing that could not be sacrificed to time and grief was the essence of the man.

"You tricked me," he said to himself, to her, to the night.

―――

190

She folded him into the fabric of herself, whispered in his ear with all the Knowledge of Silence itself. "You tricked yourself."

And he knew the truth of it. Knew he had loved her enough to throw off the chains of his mortal prison, enough to defy even the paradigm of his humanness, enough to take his first eternal breath, because turning himself rightsidewrong with the madness of love was the only cure for the fatal demon of grief.

Love is the reason and the catalyst.

Do you love yourself enough?

Possessed

> *A seeker wrote: Hollywood is making all these exorcism movies, supposedly based on true events. When I used to be a Christian, I believed it was demons, but now I am thinking it may be their mortal/human self fighting the twin because they are not aware of the twin. They will be afraid and think they are being possessed by a demon. What do you think?*

Keep in mind that Hollywood likes to say a lot of things are based on a true story when the reality of it is about as real as reality t.v.

With that said, depending on the depth of one's religious programming, what you suggest is possible. Many people have been tortured, burned at the stake and worse because of their emerging twin being mistaken for a demon. But think about it. Why would any self-respecting demon even *want* to possess a human? (This is assuming, of course that demons even exist.) It is only human ego and self-importance that makes one think one is so desirable as to be possessed from on high (or down below). The inorganics don't concern themselves with human affairs.

In reality, all humans have the ability to create the twin - but the concept is considered so off the wall in the western culture that it's easier for most people to think their loved one is possessed than to consider the possibility that there is something more to oneself than meets the eye.

It is my personal opinion that at least 99% of all cases of so-called possession are either the result of an underlying medical condition or hysterical fakery on the part of the one being "possessed." Real shamans or sorcerers or witches or prophets are quite rare.

Demons, like gods, tend not to exist unless we create them with our imagination - in which case, they are more accurately tulpas, and transient at that.

The Dark Allure

A seeker wrote: Why do you think so many are drawn to the vampyre mythos?

The vampyre mythos contains so many aspects that are intuitively alluring to the human mind/body/spirit. Think on the words "intuitively alluring". Essentially, the vampyre mythos *can* be likened to a fairy tale of sorts, which draws one in and hooks one with its imagery and its erotic underpinnings. No, I am not saying it is a fairy tale. I am saying that fairy tales arise as a way of explaining that which cannot be explained - allegory and myth painting the edges of a vast canvas of Truth which lies beyond the human's ability to perceive directly.

In the vampyre mythos, there are beings who are not only immortal, but who can theoretically create others like themselves. What is more intimate that the sharing of "blood" (animus)? What is more compelling that the idea that one could live forever, watching the centuries come and go, watching the world change? What is more darkly alluring than the notion that immortals walk among us?

This is the appeal. This is the bait to which you are drawn as moths to a flame. You feel something *more.* So close you can almost touch it, taste it, feel the gossamer wings of it on your skin.

The reality is that we are drawn to the vampyre mythos because we intuitively Know there is more to life than death. We know we have been duped and hooked into the dayshine program by well-meaning family and friends; but we sense there is something beyond the overlay, something so vast and infinitely different from what we have been taught to believe. Moreso - something that has the power to change us right down to the molecular/energetic level of our very being.

What we are really sensing is that we have the power to _be_ the very thing that compels us. Whether you call it vampyre or immortal makes little difference. It is through the arts of transformation, transcendence and transmogrification that we begin to Real-ize (make-real) the "fairy tale" which drew us to it in the first place. So the vampyre mythos remains myth only if we do not take the first step toward creating and inhabiting the totality of ourselves.

What is the totality of oneself? Simply put, it is the combined experience and highest potential of the self and the twin. The human self may be mortal, but the twin is infinite and may be anything... including vampyre, immortal, alien, elemental.

"We are the ones we have been waiting for." (Hopi proverb)

So Deep It Hurts

A seeker wrote: Several times while going about creating the twin, the ache was so deep and I felt as if I were going insane, or as if I were going to die.

The reason you feel as if you are going to die is because the twin is infinite, whereas the mortal self is finite - so it's like trying to pour the contents of the ocean into a Coke bottle. Nonetheless, it's a good experience because it illustrates to you very personally just _how_ powerful and vast the twin really is - the infinite and immortal Other. Once you have experienced that directly, it becomes virtually impossible to step off the path from that moment forward, because finally you have a glimpse of who/what you are, and you are even more compelled to create and inhabit the totality of yourself.

Many times, your twin will be gender-opposite if you are heterosexual, or gender-same if you are homosexual. Either way - I mention this because the experience of the twin is often erotic and has been described (accurately) as how it feels to fall in love so deeply in hurts.

Fall in love.

To Be Or Not To Be

A seeker wrote: I've heard that one of the bitter roots of the vampire myth is that the act of suicide would be the cause of one turning into a vampire after the crypt has closed, and cold earth is heaped upon the coffin. Western Christian culture damns souls to Hell who choose this option, while eastern cultures have endorsed and practiced it for centuries.

I will start by saying that nothing is what it seems, nothing is what you have been taught to believe. The idea of suicide as it relates to the vampire mythos is an entanglement of fact, fiction, fantasy and reality. The dayshine world mistakenly perceives that those who kill themselves rise from the dead to feed upon the living. That is the heart of the ancient myth. However, you have to ask yourself where and why the myth originated. What did the dayshine world see (or think it saw) that caused the myth to spring up in the first place? Not unlike helpless parents trying to explain sex to their children by the allegory of the birds and the bees. It's a nice fantasy, but has nothing to do with the reality of sexual intercourse.

It could be perceived that those who succeed in their bid for immortality actually do "die" to the dayshine world. As the mortal self loses its programming and embraces its immortal form (the twin), the old self "dies" as the new self emerges "from the dead." When this is perceived from a purely mundane, human perspective, all sorts of erroneous conclusions spring up and pretty soon tales are told of the wayward brother who left his home and abandoned his family and eventually "died", only to rise up from the dead and return to feed upon the living.

There are all sorts of reasons why this misperception has persisted throughout history. The dayshine society condemns that which it does not understand, and when a blanket of horror and fear can be thrown over the truth, so much the better.

As for the actuality of suicide as it may be relevant to the teachings... *I never have and never will advocate suicide.* The only possible exception would be in cases of extreme physical pain or the certainty that the end of one's life was imminent due to disease or fatal injury. Life is sacred. Every breath contains a multitude of universes and multiverses and dimensionalities beyond your ability to conceive. To obliterate even a single moment of that realm of all possibility is to destroy opportunities and experiences beyond the human mind's ability to conceive. That in itself _is_ the immortalis animus - the force of life and the _tendency_ of life to seek that next breath.

Throughout history, there have been documented cases of people who "died" and then seemingly returned from the grave. The label "vampire" is often attached to such people because it means "undead." Obviously someone who had transcended (as opposed to transformed or transmogrified) would be believed dead, but may only be in transition between one manifestation and another. The human mind cannot wrap around this in any logical manner, and so it jumps to conclusions that dear Uncle Bob has come back from the dead to eat their brains or nibble on their neck, or whatever it is the local cultural legends prescribe.

This is another reason immortals guard their identities and keep their secrets to themselves. The mortal world has no room and no tolerance for immortals, and as a result their fears have woven distorted perceptions into myths which not only feed on fear, but generate it. Why? Because as long as the song and dance can be used to distract themselves, they are spared the difficult task of stripping away their own blinders to see that the world is not what they believe, and certainly not at all what they _want_ to believe.

Pay no attention to that man behind the curtain.

Aside from the legal and moral implications of suicide, I do not feel it is a path to immortality at all. If someone is so depressed or fearful as to take their own life, they are most likely not in a frame of mind that would facilitate their evolution. This is why those who seek to become real vampyres spend years (even decades or more) training mind//body/spirit to transition from organic to inorganic with full awareness. The seeker Intends to "die awake" with awareness fully engaged, so as to avoid the fate of essentially being dis-membered and dis-integrated by the quantifiable force known in western culture as Death.

Crucifixion?
Out the door, line on the left, one cross each

A seeker wrote: Is it possible Jesus was crucified for teaching the same kind of thing we are learning here? Are the teachings themselves forbidden knowledge?

The teachings can be gleaned through gnosis by any sufficiently motivated seeker. But, yes, they are forbidden knowledge in the sense that - when taken literally and practiced diligently - they have the power to free the human mind from its slavery, and in so doing, threaten the status quo of the dayshine world. Throughout history, many "witches", shamans, and prophets have been crucified, burned at the stake and killed in lots of other nasty ways, and all because they were truthsayers accused of being soothsayers.

The dayshine world and its minions will stop at nothing to keep the matrix fully functional. It's amazing just how much the film parallels reality - up to and including Agent Smith. I've met and fought a few Agent Smiths in my time, and I can assure you they are all around you - usually waiting to jump out from behind the mask of your family members, friends and co-workers.

Have you ever seen someone suddenly possessed by the spirit of Agent Smith? If you have, then you already know the matrix is all around you and nothing is what you have been taught to believe. One moment you're talking to your dear ol' mum or dad, brother or lover... and the next moment their eyes are glazed over and they are telling you what a criminal you are for not sharing their belief in (fill in the blank) god, politics, religion, or the flat earth.

This is also why The Darker Teachings are particularly dangerous - they are like a red flag to the powers that be, because they run the high risk of freeing the mind beyond any possibility of getting that mind to go back to its comfortable slumber. Once awakened, there is no going back, so the powers that be are even more dangerous to those seekers who have moved beyond the point of Know return.

Word of warning: to anyone who wants a normal life with 2.5 nuclear children, a white picket fence and all the trappings of proper society... take the blue pill and go back to yo mama before it's too late. There is no place for you here.

Chaos Energy & Probability

In my experience, raw chaos energy is what amounts to a probability wave - energy that is not yet in use, so is therefore available for manipulation by the sorcerer or magus. The key to using chaos energy is not only defining Intent (first and foremost) but also learning the "frequency" within yourself through which to then channel that energy toward manifestation. This is where a lot of followers of "the law of attraction" get in trouble. They believe that simply wishing/hoping for something is what will cause that something to manifest (usually money or some material gain within the dayshine world). The reality is that chaos energy is moved by Will much more than even Intent. It takes Intent to manifest Will, but Will is actually the force that is the catalyst between thought and manifestation.

Example: a seeker could wish they were at Disneyland, but Will is what will put them in the car and send them on their way. Put simply, the force of Will is the bridge between intent and manifestation.

Will is the decisive movement of the molecular structure of reality itself. Think about that until it actually starts to resonate, and you'll have a good idea of how chaos energies actually work. Peter J. Carroll [12] has put math to it so that it can be seen from a quantum chaos perspective, but most seekers don't really need the math unless it is simply their desire to more fully comprehend *how* magick and science are just different perspectives of the same phenomenon. It is the force of Will that remains a mystery, and yet to those who learn how to summon it, it's not a mystery at all, but a quantum bridge between the mind of an ordinary man and the mind of a sorcerer.

---

[12] Acclaimed author of many books on the subject of chaos magick – and one of the few writers with whom *this* author generally agrees. In particular, his thoughts on "retroactive enchantment" should be required reading for anyone on this path, particularly as those ideas may relate to the creation & manifestation of one's twin.

Confronting the Matrix

A seeker wrote:
There are so many programs. How can I undo them all?

The key to destroying _all_ the programs is the Knowledge that there really is only _one_ program when all is said and done. That program is comprised of what might be called "the matrix" or "the dayshine world". Once you yank that foundation out from under yourself and really *see* that all programs are rooted in words and what those words have caused you to believe, the entirety of *all* your programs begins to crumble at the foundation.

Pick something you strongly believe and ask yourself why you believe it. Religion is often a good place to start. Or politics. When you begin to unravel not only *what* you believe, but *why* you believe it (which is usually rooted in something you have been told or read, but seldom on what you yourself have experienced) you begin to catch glimpses of The First Fundamental Lie.

But even what I have said is only words. It is only when you can go beyond the words themselves that you will truly *see*.

If you want to do a little experiment, tell me something you strongly, deeply believe, and I will dismantle it for you so you can see how the process works. A word of warning - you may not like it, because getting rid of the program can be like pulling teeth. It can be painful. What do you believe? Do you believe there is good and evil? Do you believe in a god or goddess? Do you believe in morality?

Another rule of thumb, something I wrote to an apprentice many, many years ago:

> *The surgery is delicate because the prison [The Lie] is a*
> *living entity as much as a cage and because it is such an*
> *interwoven part of you, the cutting away of the*
> *consensual disease must be performed simultaneously*
> *with the transplantation of superior replacements lest the*
> *cure destroy the patient altogether, yes?*

The same seeker wrote, in response to my challenge:
"God is good."

I'm going to start by reminding you that nothing here is personal. Then I am going to destroy your world. It may make you angry or sad. Just remember: all of these things are a choice. And do *not* make the mistake of *believing* anything I am telling you. Belief itself is nothing more than faith, and faith is the greatest destroyer of free will.

You say God is good.

I say god does not exist, and goodness is nothing more than a humanform assignation. I would ask you simply this: *why* do you believe in God in the first place? Is it something you were taught by parents or teachers? Is it something you read in a book? Go back as far as you can and really examine where this belief came from. Were you told the typical fairy tales of a caring father-figure on a throne, looking down upon his human children? Do you understand that this is the explanation parents generally give in the western culture when the child begins to become aware of its mortality? Ah, but do you also understand that even mortality is part of the larger consensus which tells you, "All things die"?

This is a good place to observe that all programs are deeply interconnected. As the child begins to question, the parents generally want to offer comfort or some sense of continuity that transcends all logic. So the child is indoctrinated with the prevailing belief system of its culture - in this case, Christianity. You were *told* that God exists, but you have never seen him. You may even *believe* God exists, but there is a crucial difference between what you believe and what you really Know. You may believe aliens from Alpha Centauri are creating crop circles in your shaving cream, but that doesn't make it so. The *only* way to Know would be to experience it directly - and I am willing to bet you have not experienced "god" directly. If you think you have, I am willing to bet you are merely drawing erroneous conclusions based on what you (again) have been told, and have come to passively believe.

Erroneous conclusions. This is another area where the seeker has to be extremely aware. A magnificent sunset or a remission from cancer is not evidence of the existence of God. So if you plan on using the argument of "I just feel God exists and therefore I know God exists..." think again. What you feel is largely rooted in biochemical exchanges in the brain or programming/conditioning that has been placed upon you by well-meaning parents, teachers, friends. Do you realize you are culturally programmed to recoil from a spider or snake, and feel warmth toward a butterfly or kitten? And in the exact same way, you have been programmed to believe "God is good," when the reality is that there is no proof of God and no proof of goodness. Both exist as concepts in your mind - ideas that represent something which does not exist.

As a brief aside, the idea of "goodness" might come one centimetre closer to reality than the idea of god - only because it has been proven that all humans (with the possible exception of sociopaths) have within themselves a barometer which tells us right from wrong at a very intuitive level. This has nothing to do with social standards or morality. It has to do with survival instinct. For example, you know instinctively not to stick your hand in fire or try to breathe underwater. Bad things will happen, and so this level of programming exists under the heading of "instinct".

Tribal cultures will tell you that their warriors know intuitively not to kill a pregnant doe or hunt the buffalo to extinction. None of these things have any connection to the idea of goodness, but fall under a broader heading of what Carlos Castaneda referred to as "the right way to live." As it was stated in Harry Potter, "There is no good or evil, only power." The fact that the line was delivered by the "evil" Voldemort" is irrelevant. It is an undeniable statement of fact. Go(o)d and (D)evil do not exist, except as extensions of human beliefs.

If you have any doubt of this, take the concept one step further. What would "good" look like? Is it a gaseous cloud or a scoop of ice cream or a mantra mumbled on the lips of monks? What does evil look like? Is it a demon with an appetite for little children, or a serial killer preying on the weak? As you take this further and further down the rabbit hole, what you will discover is that good and evil, god and devil, are _all_ only creations of Man, and not the other way around. Man created God in his own image because Man realizes intuitively that he is mortal and seeks something outside of himself to save him. Sadly, Man _is_ God, but the moment Man takes responsibility for that huge responsibility, all of Man's comfort zones are wiped out in a nano-second, and he comes face to face with himself in the mirror. But instead of seeing his intrinsic power and ability, Man usually sees only his limitations and fears, and so he sings the world into being as the illusory dream-state wherein this extant "god" exists who will somehow reach into the illusion and pluck the soul of Man out of harm's way, and into a world where the streets are paved with gold atop the big rock candy mountain.

Sound like a fairy tale? That's because it is.

When you say "God is good," you reveal that you are still operating inside the humanform program at a very base level. The first step toward real freedom (immortality, transmogrification, however you want to label it) requires the seeker to eradicate _any_ belief which places responsibility outside himself. If you believe in God, you are automatically saddled with _all_ of the programming that goes with it - all of the illusions and lies and comfort zones Man has created in an attempt to abdicate responsibility for his own salvation. By accepting one aspect of the God program, you accept the whole program, even if you are not aware of it. Why? Because the idea of God predisposes one to believe in an extant deity who must be called upon and/or appeased in some way, and only then will this God intervene on one's behalf.

Extant. Outside. Separate. Apart. And, as a result, supremely disempowering.

As long as Man places God outside himself, Man has given away his power and relinquished his ability to save himself. The Catholics and others have depended on this for centuries, and if you think for a moment that it is a benevolent belief system, think again. The church depends on keeping people ignorant and dependent - because that's what keeps the money rolling in to the church coffers.

Is this good? Is this God?

If God is good, why would he allow such travesty in his name? Would a truly benevolent and loving God of goodness allow wars to be fought in his name? If you try to tell me, "God works in mysterious ways," then you are even more hopeless than you may realize. That is just the standardized lingo which translates to, "Pay no attention to that man behind the curtain." As long as you can go on believing in the Great & Powerful Oz, you don't need to look down and see that you've been wearing the ruby slippers all along. As long as you can be blinded and hoodwinked by the razzle-dazzle of God, you are failing to see that the only God that exists is the one staring back at you over the sink every morning when you brush your teeth.

Think about it. If you think God is good, then you must think it is good that sexual predators prey on children, or animals are tortured by madmen who film themselves doing all sorts of heinous deeds just for the sake of doing it. Is this goodness? If God exists, would he allow such things? We could argue about free will and choice, but the bottom line is that _if_ God exists, and _if_ you accept that s/he created all things, then god created the serial killer _knowing_ that person would become a serial killer, and God created the 7-year old girl who will be brutalized and raped by the serial killer, _knowing_ that would be her fate.

If you still think "God is good," then I would bet you really aren't thinking. You are basing your statement on a pre-existing belief that has nothing to do with reality. Or you are drawing erroneous conclusions based on wishful thinking.

A man looks up at the sky and sees a falling star. "What a magnificent miracle from God!" he exclaims.

On the other side of the world, that falling star turns out to be a wayward meteorite that crashes into a village, killing hundreds. "What an evil act of vengeance from the gods!" the women who lost 3 children cries.

It's all in how you _see_ it.

There is no god. There is no goodness. There is no truth.

You create the world through what you believe. Just be sure you are creating a world you want to live in.

Dispelling the Myths

> _A seeker wrote: What are your thoughts on the idea of Hell? How does it relate to the vampire mythos?_

There are so many levels of allegory at this stage of the vampire mythos that it would take volumes to untangle them all. But suffice it to say, the "vampire" has become a caricature of the truth that lies underneath. For example, the idea that the vampire casts no reflection comes from the much darker reality -

the vampyre's reflection is his/her twin. Most humans cannot fathom that they are actually a trinity (self, twin, totality), and so they create simple-minded explanations to staunch their own fears. Easier for the humans to blame the vampire than to understand that real Vampyres are evolved humans who walk the earth the same as anyone else.

Humans are masters of rendering what they don't understand down to the lowest common denominator - the vampire is said to have no reflection, therefore he has no soul. Where's the logic in that? The vampyre has *created* his soul and it is off in the bends and bubbles of space and beyond the illusion of time, living 10,000 lifetimes in the span of an instant, gathering Knowledge and experience, all of which are how the Vampyre is created in the first place - it's a moebius loop. Humans, of course, know nothing of quantum moebius loops, much preferring to sit in front of the tv fretting over what to ask their doctor, and what inane reality tv show they are going to watch next.

In some of my shamanic journeys many years ago, I observed some of what was described in Dante's Inferno, and what might be considered the Biblical version of Hell. What I concluded is that Hell is a sort of eternal limbo for those who don't complete their evolution sufficiently to inhabit the totality of themselves. It isn't a place of punishment created by or for anyone else. It is simply the fragmented soul's tormented perception. Humans depict it as eternal flames because death by fire is one of the most frightening things humans can envision. But the Hells I have observed (and visited) are fragmented segments of awareness that result when a human fails to evolve. This has been rendered down to the notion that one is being punished for sins against god – lowest common denominator thinking. Purgatory is nothing more than awareness without cohesion.

Those who never make the attempt to evolve are reabsorbed into the fabric of all possibility and start over as something else - just the universe recycling itself. Hell seems to be more a state of torment for those who "try" and don't make it. Most commonly, seekers may reach a certain level of awareness and then either try to go back to the matrix, or decide they've "done enough." What this results in is a partially-formed twin and an unevolved mortal. The end result? Limbo. Or, as humans prefer to say... Hell.

This is one of the darker aspects or the darker teachings, and it's something I don't often like to address because it can have a rather heart-stopping effect if one looks at it too closely, though it is obvious even if you're *not* looking. Simply put: there really is a point of no return from which you can't go back to the comfort zones of the matrix. Or, more precisely, you can go back to the roles and the pretences of normal life but you will have been so fundamentally changed that you can't un-remember what you have learned. You have been changed at a fundamental level - at the level of your own quantum existence.

Those who reach that level really don't have the luxury of quitting or going off to seek another path. Why? Because there is no other path. There are other belief systems and other models of consciousness, but there is only one path when all is said and done. It is the path that connects the dots between the mortal self and the immortal Other - and once you go more than a few steps down that road, you have taken onto yourself the responsibility for your twin in the same way you would take on yourself the responsibility for a child. If you abandon it along the way, you not only abandon your chance for immortality, you also potentially condemn yourself to this idea of "eternal torment" which has been rendered down by human mis-understanding to the idea of hell.

The good news is that even Hell can be transcended, but best not to go there in the first place.

"Do. Or do not. There is no try." (Yoda)

As always, my answers are just words in an ocean of languages, all of which are illusions.

For the Sake of Love, I Am Divided
The twin is the manifestation of what you desire – not only what you desire as a mate and a companion, but what you desire of yourself. Your energies become entangled, eventually to such a degree that there is no difference between twin and self, but those words are uttered with caution and caveats, lest you think the process is automatic rather than Intended. It is like this: when you call out to the night and the stars and the vampyres hiding inside the edges of autumn, when you wrap your words up in fallen leaves rushing down a lonesome road and ask them to

carry the wishes of witches into the infinite, what you are doing is telling your twin who and what you need him to be. At first it is like a tiny seed, just an inkling that tickled your fancy when you were a child, staring out the window in school, watching the wind in the trees while the teacher prattled about Dick and Jane and all the other petty illusions.

The twin is what you need him to be. More than that, as the twin is developed through long-term intent, he becomes the force that stands at your back, whispering in your ear all the ingredients that are necessary for his creation. This is where the mortal and the twin swear a sacred pact which can never broken if both are to survive into eternity. For this is when the twin takes his first breath and becomes the I-Am in eternity. This is where the egg divides in an evolutionary mitosis so that it will be always driven to come together again, recreating in eternity what was begun within the mortal dream.

When I say the egg divides, what I mean is this. Until the double takes his first breath, there is only the mortal self. That mortal self, if she is destined to become an immortal, goes through a process of longing, needing, aching, and feelings which lead her to be always impressing upon the universe itself the thoughtform of that-which-will-cure-the-hurt. As a child, perhaps the cure was seen as a cartoon hero in your dreams who came to rescue you from nightmares and dayshine bullies. As a young girl blossoming into her witchy womanhood, perhaps the paradigm shifted to a vampyre king, plucked from the heart of your imaginings and imbued with the power of blessed immortality. As you have grown, so has he, and what is important to understand is that it is always the need that fuels the flame. When you stop needing, you stop creating. When there is no more poetic longing in your heart, there are no more poems on the page.

Words, stabbing at the nothing, hitting only the infinite walls of the abyss. What it means is this: the egg divides for love. There is a saying in Zen: *for the sake of love I am divided so that I might forever seek reunion.* So it is with the twin. This is the nature of vampyre transformation that transcends the space time continuum. This is where the desires of the heart are written in blood on the fabric of the universe, and brought into being through the awful ache and pain of the will birthing that which the heart has summoned into being. There are no words for this, and so you must look at it carefully, from the corner of the third eye, and never in direct light which can chase the magick away.

The twin is a culmination of the desires of a lifetime, but because it is not constrained by time, it can hop in and out of your dreams, from the time you are capable of remembering. Mortals live within a finite box, whereas once the twin is created from *any* assemblage point *inside* that box, the twin then moves outside the box and begins to function as what might be perceived as an independent force, often stretching back to your earliest memories. You will be forever drawn to that which you have created, and it will take on many manifestations. But what is vital to comprehend is that all of it hinges on this ongoing creation, for there is no way to be absolutely certain when the twin's first breath is taken, and so if you falter in your journey before that moment in the linear now, it is possible for the twin to disappear and the mortal self to lapse back into phantomhood.

This is why you must be forever caught in the throes of self-creation, the birthing pains of conception, so that he *can* exist as all those things that have shaped your life. He is telling you how to create him, by pointing you in the direction of the very things which make your heart ache with the force of creation.

Chaos Magick and the Twin

The twin is not something that exists by default. It is something *created* by what might be loosely defined (very loosely) as "chaos magick." So those who speak of the higher self as if it is a given are sadly mistaken - we are not born with it, we summon it into being with the force of energy and will. The human organism is capable of creating and then projecting the twin beyond the organic form. In that way, the inorganic twin becomes the vessel of awareness when the organic form is shed. Ultimately, you create the twin (or not). You project it (or not). You inhabit it (or not). Because it is not confined by the limitations of the space-time continuum once it is projected, it may serve as teacher/guide/mentor - ergo... "You have to *be* immortal before you will know how to *become* immortal."

For those initially seeking to create the double/other/twin... to put this in terms of chaos magick, it is no different than any other magickal process, at least at a fundamental level. The key element is *desire*, fueled by love. The twin cannot be created from an intellectual perspective alone. Most people who take this path toward transformation, transcendence or transmogrification do it because they are compelled to do it. Some say it is the unborn twin pulling them - in a quantum universe where time has no meaning, this is entirely likely. Others believe the compulsion is simply an expression of our human potential for evolution - for the twin is the energetic vessel that is the Self beyond the organic continuum. I must stress that we are not born with this, as most religions would have you believe. It is something that is created in the process of living, *in the process of listening to the demands of the heart.* It is why children have invisible friends, it is why every human has daydreamed about his/her "perfect match". It is why we are here: to create the part of ourselves that is immortal and eternal, above and beyond the organic dayshine world.

Religions prefer to teach (because it's easier to understand, even if entirely incorrect) that we have this thing called the "soul" that is somehow magically injected into the fetus at the moment of conception. The reality - harsh and ugly but true - is that we are little more than organic meat suits until such time as we feel the first inklings which tell us we are beings who are going to die. Think back on your life. When did you first encounter the concept of death? What did that do to you? Did you suddenly realize that this magnificent mystery could simply stop, and that your entire world would end with your final breath? If you are like most seekers, even at an early age you found this concept not only alien and strange, but altogether unacceptable. It is that feeling of indignation that causes most seekers to begin weaving the tapestry of the twin at an early age. This is the natural process of human evolution - because the end result is that this is where/how the mortal self begins to create and project beyond himself the energetic construct (a thought-form at first) that eventually becomes the full-fledged twin.

If you believe for a single moment that your continuity beyond this life is a given (whether heaven or hell or purgatory or the fields of Elysium), you have been suckered into the human program and need to seriously examine your belief systems. The soul is a myth as it is generally explained, for the same reason past lives are a myth as they are generally mis-perceived.

When you really look at life, it's fairly easy to see this - though the cultural/social programming runs so deep most cannot get beyond the idea that they are entitled to a soul/twin just by virtue of being born – one of the most fundamentally difficult programs the mortal self has to undo before s/he can have sufficient motivation to begin the magickal process of self-creation.

These terms are clinical and not particularly exciting. That is why I prefer poetry to the sterility of intellectual debate, but occasionally it's necessary to throw back the curtains and take a long, hard look at what is hiding behind them.

I should also stress that the twin can be anything you Will it to be - vampyre, vulcan, pirate, prince, pauper, king. The sorcerer's trick is to project the twin in such a way that it has the ability to transcend the natural order of life/death. Wouldn't make much sense to create your twin as a sickly mortal oaf.

Remember: the twin is not confined by the rules & limitations of the mortal, dayshine world. You can Be anything you can imagine.

But take care, and remember: love is the reason. Without it, the twin is only a fleeting reflection, dying in the womb. If you cannot fall in love with your twin, you cannot project him/her into the infinite. And it is only when the twin is projected beyond the organic self that s/he gains the power and wisdom to teach you how to create him/her in the first place.

Put very simply: the twin begins as a thoughtform, usually at an early age though not always. That thought-form is comprised of energy (*your* energy), and if it is nurtured with love and fed with animus (lifeforce), it grows in strength and wisdom until it takes on a life of its own wherein it is ubiquitous throughout the space-time continuum and beyond. It exists simultaneously in the year 1000 BC and the year 100,000 AD, and is the vessel which experiences what are commonly called past lives, but which are really parallel movements of the double within the infinite sphere of the Now.

My twin once said to me... "You created me to create you." That is the essence of quantum vampyre magick.

I dreamed you into Be-ing
and gave you half my heart.
You took it, bleeding,
to vampyreland
so I would be always drawn there,
moth to flame, moon to night,
heart to beat.
You are the reflection
who fled from the mirror.

The Meaning of Life

A seeker wrote (in response to the segment above):
I am deeply troubled to the point of near panic regarding
your comment that we are not born with a soul.

If I have the power to plunge your existence into chaos, then it
was never stable to begin with. I say that not to be cruel, but to
impress upon you the realization that you are being given a great
gift through this experience - not from anything I have said or
done, but through your own inner awakening. When I say you
have to create your own soul, I mean that quite literally. The fact
that you are in such distress tells me you are well on your way to
doing so - but like every other seeker, you must go through the
process, painful and frightening though it can be at times. If it
were easy, everybody would do it - and the sad reality is that
most never even take the first step. Instead, they cling to their
comforting beliefs (whether deities, angels, spirits or total
atheism), because it will always be easier to just go on believing
what makes one happy as opposed to digging deeper for the
thing(s) that will make one secure.

Secure? Aha. Therein lies the rub.

Do you know why humans are half mad? Do you know why they
suffer? Because they are aware of their mortality, their transient
nature, their fragile and short organic existence. What would
soothe that fear? What would make one feel secure again?
Simply put - the Knowledge that one need not succumb to the
programs and the agreements. Obviously this is not something
that can be gained by wishing for it or hoping for it (as in the so-
called "law of attraction"). It can only be gained through direct
personal experience - the process of awakening, followed by the
process of undoing the programs, followed by the process of

assimilation... and finally sealed with the process of transformation, transcendence or transmogrification.

It is in the do-ing of these processes that one creates and projects the twin - which becomes the inorganic vessel for awareness beyond the threshold of Death, whether that threshold comes through transformation, transcendence or transmogrification. Where does the soul come in? Simple. The mortal self is the source of the twin - not the other way around, despite what a lot of religious and spiritual traditions would have you believe. Once the mortal self begins to awaken (whether as a child or on one's deathbed at the age of 95), s/he is filled with an energy that can only be likened to the quantifiable force of Love.

I do not mean love in some quasi-romantic breeder instinct, but in the sense that love is an indefinable force that re-creates the human self at a higher frequency than where it previously resided. Put another way - love at this level is transformative in and of itself, and so it is the catalyst from which The Work progresses. This is the kind of love that transcends all other - you might call it unconditional love, but I find it more helpful to think of it as love of Life itself. The love affair one has with being alive - the reason the organism is compelled to take that next breath even when one may think his/her ordinary life is dull or uninspired. At a much deeper level of awareness, one Knows Life is a rare and beautiful lover, even if occasionally cruel.

There is only you and your Intent and your free will to re-create yourself from moment to moment. Immortals are connected at the molecular level to the energetic web from which all things are made manifest. Mortals are made of the same material, but have lost their direct connection to the web. The trick is in re-establishing the connection that is as natural as breathing. That connection is through the living soul, which is the bridge between mortal self and immortal twin.

Take back your power. Breathe in life and love and breathe out intent and will. This is how you are born into the Life that never ends.

We are here to experience Life, and to be in love with it. And that in itself is when and where and why the soul takes its first breath - in the realization that Life is love and love is life.

———

210

GLOSSARY

ABYSS: 1) The emptiness or the nothing, the absence of all things. Most people have never seen the abyss, while others think of it (erroneously) as the religious vision of "hell". If consciousness is existence, the abyss is oblivion. 2) The hollow emptiness inside someone who has made no attempt at their own personal evolution. The soulless void. In this definition, the abyss is the pit of despair into which people fall when they experience what is traditionally called a "loss of faith". Fortunately, it is this loss of faith and the subsequent fall into the abyss from which the journey toward evolution often begins. When faith fails or is intentionally abandoned, it is from the abyss that we begin our climb toward self-identity and self-Realization.

ANIMUS: Lifeforce. The ghost inside the machine. The inexplicable breath which separates life from death. Pure energy.

ASSEMBLAGE POINT (or AP) – The assemblage point the viewpoint through which we see our world. Some perceive the assemblage point as a physical location on the body, between the shoulder blades, but other mystics & seers view it simply as the automatic "program" which runs in the background of our minds once we have been fully socialized into the world - normally at around age 4. It is through learning to move the assemblage point that the seeker may begin to experience the reality of other perceptions, other "worlds", the immortal kingdom. The assemblage point also moves of its accord in times of physical or emotional duress. An assemblage point that is out of alignment results in dis-ease and states of unwellness which may encompass mind, body & spirit equally or individually.

ASSIMILATION: The synthesis of information into a personal system of knowledge. Taking the pieces of the puzzle (the teachings) not just at face value, but as a well-tested Whole. Assimilation is the process of taking what you have learned and weaving it into the foundation of your own unique individuation. Follow no one. Believe nothing. Test everything. This is the act of assimilation. It cannot be done in a single night, but is a long-term commitment to the evolution of consciousness.

BELIEF SYSTEM - Any school of thought which requires belief or faith as opposed to personal experience. One example: Christianity. Another example: Atheism. Both require belief in external forces or causes, and are therefore only opposing sides of the same coin. Christianity requires faith that God exists. Atheism requires the belief that there is no God. Ultimately, neither the Christian nor the atheist can prove his beliefs, so faith of one sort or another is required in either point of view, and therefore both systems fail as vehicles to Knowledge.

BRUTE WITH THE SCYTHE: Death.

CLARITY: The heightened perception of seeing things as they truly are, without the usual clutter of ideas and belief systems. Clarity is intrinsic to seers, but must be sought & practiced by those who have not yet achieved the ability to see. Do not mistake what you believe for what you see. Clarity is the ability to know the difference.

COHESION OF IDENTITY - a state of being in which the seeker has gained a sense of self-awareness beyond all programs - i.e., the seeker knows who he or she is apart from who they are related to, or what they do for a living. When the seeker has achieved cohesion, it is then possible to inhabit the Whole self into eternity as a singularity of consciousness. This is also a definition of the immortal condition.

CONSENSUAL REALITY or CONSENSUS REALITY or CONSENSUAL CONTINUUM – the world of ordinary dayshine awareness, defined & shaped by what is agreed-upon by the majority of the consensus. The Real World. The societies, cultures and definitions of "reality" we take for granted, and upon which we all agree as to what is real and what is fantasy, what is right and what is wrong. We are indoctrinated into the consensual reality from the moment we are born, primarily through language, and yet it can be proven through simple observation that much of this indoctrination is incorrect, that what is "right" to one culture is "wrong" to another, that what is "normal" to one consensus is abhorrent to another. We live, therefore, in a world of illusions, a world of words, even a world of lies. Knowing this gives the seeker the power to think outside the box and move outside the illusion.

DAYSHINE WORLD - The world of ordinary awareness, everyday life. The play. The matrix. It should be understood that most seekers have a dayshine life of one type or another. Meaning: we all feed at some level on the real world until we evolve. Our dayshine lives would include job, family, friends, everything that is of the 'real' world. It is no shame to have a dayshine life. It is only a shame if that is the _only_ life we have. Immortal vampyres live a duality. See 'duality'.

DOUBLE (aka "twin") – For practical purposes, the double is the self in eternity, but can be visualized as the vessel into which the seeker uploads his consciousness and identity through the process of self-creation. All seekers can develop a double, though most remain unaware of the existence of the double. The double is the energy body personified, developed through Intent and Dreaming to a point of extreme cohesion. The double may take on a life of its own. The double is also known as the energy body, the vampyre twin, the higher self. It may or may not look like the humanform self. Many doubles are opposite-gender and also serve the role as muse, teacher, mentor, benefactor.

DREAMING - in the magickal world, "dreaming" is an artform which cannot be explained in a few brief words. It is an active application of intent which enables the seeker to dream lucidly and navigate the dreamscape in much the same way we navigate the terrain of our ordinary dayshine awareness. Through impeccable dreaming, the vampyre twin is created, and through dreaming the seeker begins to explore shifts of the assemblage point which enable her to assemble other worlds. Through dreaming, it becomes possible to connect the worlds of heightened awareness with the world of ordinary awareness - or put another way, to enter the night that never ends at will.

———

DREAMING AWAKE – a level of awareness wherein the seeker enters a state of dreaming while remaining technically in a state of first attention awareness. To those who have experienced it, no explanation is necessary. To those who have not, no explanation is possible.

DUALITY - Meaning, literally, "two things simultaneously". This is not the same thing as dualism, which implies perception through opposites (i.e., dualism is the human propensity for perceiving black/white, good/evil, god/devil, male/female, etc) Duality implies the evolving perception which enables us to see that past and future are no different, but only different perceptions according to our location in time. Duality further allows for two seemingly contradictory conditions to exist simultaneously, without either obliterating or in any way usurping the other. Example: "a love/hate relationship". Another example: We exist as mortal human beings in the Now, and simultaneously as eternal beings through the energy body of the double. Duality can be studied in the statement, "You must *be* immortal before you will know how to *become* immortal."

ETERNAL BEING - An evolved consciousness that has gathered its cohesion into Wholeness, and exists ubiquitously throughout the space-time continuum and beyond. The eternal being may project an energy body which would be indistinguishable from a corporeal body if that were the Intent, or be entirely non-corporeal, strictly as a matter of Will.

(The) FALL: The transition between mortality and immortality. In traditional vampyre symbolism, the death of the mortal self in the arms of his/her vampyre-creator, which opens the door to the immortal condition. Keep in mind, however, that symbolism is only that. The fall is the corridor between life and death, between mortal and immortal. It may take many forms. Some survive the fall. Most don't. If you're going to fall, best you have wings to fly.

FIRST FUNDAMENTAL LIE (The): The human paradigm is built on the false notion of Time, and so it could be observed by one outside of the matrix that the entire paradigm itself is erroneous because it has created within its subjects a viewpoint that is based on what immortals call The First Fundamental Lie. Think on this, for it is only when you are willing to sacrifice The Lie that you will be able to glimpse these fundamental elements of creation which are channeled through your essential be-ing pure and limitless, but limited entirely by The Lie which was seemingly designed to do just that. You are made of the pixels and photons of limitlessness and timelessness, yet unable to access that nature because the nature of any consensus is to create parameters which can only limit the power and understanding of the thing itself.

FOLLY: Anything which does not advance the seeker toward his goal of immortality may be seen as folly. Dalliances in dayshine dramas.

FOREIGN INSTALLATION, COLLECTIVE MIND, SOCIAL MIND: If it can be perceived that the consensual reality possesses a rudimentary hive mind, it then becomes possible to see that this hive mind is predatory in nature, in that it invades and usurps the individual unless the individual has mastered extreme awareness - also known as 'individuation'. Humans are largely governed by the consensual hive, whose primary agenda is to preserve its status quo. Other definitions have been offered for the predatory mind, and may have truth as well. Some believe the foreign installation is sentient. However, most immortals *see* it for what it is: a deeply-imbedded program designed to keep the hive members docile and compliant with the program itself.

GHOST TRAIN: a peculiar interaction between mortal self and immortal twin. After the mortal has created his twin, should he fail to achieve transmogrification, there is a theory which states that the fully-developed twin has the ability to step back in time to a point when the mortal self was still in the mother's womb. By entering the mortal self prior to birth, the vampyre twin is then "born" into the same body as the mortal self – the agenda being to enforce the mortal self's evolution by essentially existing as the internal teacher. For anyone with an understanding of quantum mechanics, this is not so far-fetched, since time is not linear but actually a sphere, where all events are non-local. Put simply, the 'ghost train' runs back and forth on the same track until such time as the mortal self and vampyre twin conjoin to create the singularity/totality of both.

GNOSIS: Silent knowing; communication with the higher self and the sentient universe. A state of consciousness accessible through a wide variety of methods, including but not limited to simple Intent, meditation, certain mind-altering substances such as psilocybin mushrooms, tantric sex, the near-death-experience (or NDE), sensory deprivation, and many other methods. Gnosis is the most crucial tool available to the seeker, for it is through gnosis that the entire knowledge of the entire universe is available. What matters is that when the universe speaks, we not only listen, but apply our full Intent to the task of discovering the meaning behind the words. As our abilities & awareness increase, we may begin to have a permanent channel to the voice of gnosis through our connection to our own immortal twin.

GRID: The energetic framework upon which reality hangs. Put simply, the universe is comprised of energy. For seers, that energy may be observed as a 'grid' which often appears bright green. It is the rearranging of that energy which results in our experience of reality. We hang our lives on the grid, for example. The structure of all the worlds hangs on the grid. All things are made of energy, including the grid itself. It is believed by some that the grid is the game board on which the impersonal universe plays out its game plan. Impersonal - without compassion, thought or agenda.

HEIGHTENED AWARENESS: a state of increased perception, wherein the seeker can learn and assimilate far more rapidly and deeply than from within ordinary awareness. One of the tasks of the seeker is to "remember the other self", (put another way: the act of remembering the other self is the process of creating the twin) which consists in part of bringing into ordinary awareness the events s/he has experienced in this altered state of consciousness. Humans simply do not possess the preceptor organs of memory for events that occurred in heightened awareness, just as we cannot see the subatomic world with the naked eye. Special tools are required – in this case, the tools of perception.

IMMORTAL BEING or IMMORTAL - The terms "immortal" and "eternal being" and "real vampyre" are used somewhat interchangeably unless specifically noted otherwise, though by strict definition there is considerable difference. On the evolutionary scale, it could be surmised that an eternal being or "real vampyre" has fewer limitations than an immortal still attached to organic form. Picture this: if a comet smashes the earth and the planet is reduced to rubble, the eternal being or real vampyre has the option of simply manifesting elsewhere, becoming entirely formless, or assembling other worlds. The physical immortal, on the other hand, might not have as many options, depending on the level of evolution of consciousness.

IMMORTAL CONDITION: A state of being which has transcended organic form. The immortal condition is a quantum state in which individuated consciousness & awareness would be attached to an energetic vessel as opposed to an organic one. Real vampyres have achieved the immortal condition. Other possible manifestations would include the faerie kingdom, shape-shifters, skinwalkers and far more. For the sake of this book, however, when the immortal condition is invoked, it may normally be taken to mean a real vampyre.

IMMORTAL VAMPYRE: A being who has attained the immortal condition, through the process of transmogrification. True immortal vampyres do not drink blood, sleep in coffins, or any of the usual Hollywood projections. Many may *choose* to engage a certain 'vampire lifestyle' for purely personal or aesthetic reasons, but the truth is that real vampyres walk among us in daylight and in the night, and unless it was their intent, you could not distinguish them from any other (seemingly) human being. The immortal vampyre is a transformed human - meaning that s/he is no longer confined within the limits of an organic body, but has instead attained a quantum state wherein s/he might rightly be called an "energy being" or (ironically) a being of light.

INDIVIDUATION – The manifestation of the Self as a singularity of consciousness, or eternal being. The foundation of the immortal condition is individuation. Many paths teach unity within the all as a goal of the afterlife, whereas Individuation is the act of maintaining the unique and individual I-Am throughout eternity.

INTENT – Intent (or "unbending intent") could be loosely defined as an idea or thought-form held constantly in the seeker's mind until it becomes a literal part of the seeker himself. Thought = energy. For example, it is my intent to achieve the immortal condition, which will enable me to exist as a cohesive, sentient being with a single point of view continuing into eternity. The strength of that unbending intent determines the manner in which the seeker lives, which paths are taken.

INTERNAL DIALOG: The voice of The Program, running inside your head. It is the voice that sings the world into being with its observations, but also the voice that condemns, controls and conspires to keep the human organism in alignment with the program itself. It is the voice that plays songs in your head to disrupt deeper thinking. It is the static running in the background, filled with doubts, fears, judgments, self-recriminations, and mindless chatter. It is the soundtrack which prevents you from hearing the voice of the higher self (the voice of gnosis).

KNOWLEDGE - as used throughout these documents, Knowledge shall refer to the result of direct personal experience. Example: we are taught as children that fire will burn, but until we touch a candle flame to see for ourselves, we cannot know for sure. The vampyre candidate seeks Knowledge, never settling for faith or belief systems. The greatest Knowledge comes through gnosis.

LETHE: The River of Forgetting.

LIFEFORCE: Lifeforce is energy and it is all around us at all times. One common vampire myth is that lifeforce may only be found in the blood of humans. Incorrect - and those who make the mistake of believing that myth may find themselves dead, imprisoned, or worse. Bottom line: "real vampyres" don't drink blood - neither animal, human nor otherwise. (There are exceptions, of course, largely related to sexual stimulation - but for all practical purposes, it must be understood that immortals feed on lifeforce, not physical blood.) Lifeforce may also be known as prana, chi, ki, pneuma or mana. In the quantum universe, it is ingested or absorbed through the force of Will, most often driven by desire.

MAGICK or MAGIC – Magick is the force within the human organism which enables us to do, perceive and interact with things for which science has no immediate explanation. It is the force which enables a 110 pound woman to lift a 5,000 pound truck off her child in a crisis. It is the force that we recognize as "the little voice" that tells a man not to get onboard a doomed airliner. It is the ghost inside the machine, and it is altogether human. One day, science will explain "magick", and yet magick will never be fully understood, for as we grow and evolve, our magick grows & evolves with us – like the muse, always one step ahead so we will always be compelled to follow. Magick is not defined by adherence to ritual or religion. Magick is the force being sought through certain rituals, but magick itself is most definitely not ritual or religion any more than "the soul" can be found in "the church". At best, one is only a tool used in searching for the other.

MULTIVERSE: Multiple universes, alternate or parallel dimensions. These "otherwheres" may be accessed at Will once the seeker has attained the immortal condition. Prior to that, such otherwheres may be accessed through Dreaming or astral travel. For example: what are commonly believed to be past lives are actually other positions of the Self within the Dreaming body. What the hell does that mean, you ask? Simply this: if it is the Intent of your mortal self to attain the immortal condition, you may already be a vampyre or other immortal being in one or more of these multiverses/parallel dimensions. The task for the mortal self is learning to project into one's immortal core-identity - so as to open one's eyes inside the Dream, become the immortal self, and in doing so, embrace the totality of Oneself.

NEGATIVE PLEASANTRY: Feeling good about feeling bad. Enjoying your depression or illness or dis-ability? Ask yourself what you're getting out of it. The answers might enlighten you.

NIGHT THAT NEVER ENDS: An advanced perception. the night that never ends is a quantum state in which time no longer exists. The seeker enters into perpetual night even though the dayshine world goes on all around him. For those who See, no further explanation is necessary. For those who do not yet See, no further explanation is possible, but may be attained as the seeker advances through The Work.

NON-LOCAL WEB OF INFORMATION: Essentially, the sentient but impersonal universe at large. All knowledge and all recorded experience exists within the non-local web of information, and may be accessed through gnosis.

ORDINARY AWARENESS: The normal human range of perception, which includes the 5 physical senses. The lowest common denominator of human awareness.

OVERLAY - (see also consensual reality) Essentially, the overlay is the "play" of which we are all a part. It is the dayshine lives we live and the things we do which we mistake for real, but which are only extensions of the human-default program - the dayshine world. If we could see the world with the innocence of a newborn child or an alien being who knows nothing of the human paradigm, we would see the world as it really is - without all the automatic things we say, think and do because it is intrinsically programmed into us. Evolving our perception beyond the overlay is the first step toward entering the night that never ends.

PETTY TYRANT: Anyone in a position of authority,, but particularly someone who lords their authority over another. Example: an unreasonable boss or a domineering partner or parent. Petty tyrants should be seen as gifts – examples of what must be overcome through the art of simply letting go.

PHANTOM - Individuals still plugged into the belief systems of the consensual reality. Phantoms define themselves by what they do, the company they keep, the church they attend, their social status. Another mark of a phantom is that they possess an unlimited number of personalities and roles, all without the cohesion of a single, unified "I-Am". Phantoms are organic machines within the larger machine. Are you a phantom or an authentic spirit?

PROGRAM - The information which we accept as truth without confirming or disproving it for ourselves. For example, we are taught, "All things die," and because this would appear to be true, most people accept the statement as fact rather than doing their own quest for Knowledge into the veracity or falseness of the statement itself. In reality, we cannot know for certain that "all things die." We can only know what our perceptions reveal to us within our immediate environment. By altering our perceptions - thereby altering our automatic expectations (the program) - we learn to see that much of what we think we "know" about the world is only what we "believe". The danger of all programs is that as long as they are accepted blindly as fact, they prevent us from exploring other possibilities. If, for example, the Wright Brothers had accepted the program-du-jour which stated, "Man is not meant to fly," we would live in a vastly different world.

QUANTUM UNIVERSE: We no longer live in a world of matter and energy, but a multiverse of matter/energy - in short, the two concepts are no longer separate, but halves of a whole. So what? The essential core of the immortal condition is that the immortal is entirely free of the belief/program which tells us we are comprised of matter, and that all things die. In the quantum universe, we are beings of energy. The trick to achieving the immortal condition is to make that Real-ization actual and REAL. The quantum universe allows for this through the process known as transmogrification. Put simply: energy may assemble into any apparent form. When one thinks this through, the potentials are enormous. We are no longer bound by prisons of flesh, but may instead embrace the immortal condition through the Willful transference from physical body into energy (or dreaming) body.

REAL-IZE: In terms of magick, to make real. To manifest, whether physical or mental. To bring forth rather than merely conceptualize.

RETROACTIVE ENCHANTMENT: A term probably coined by Peter J. Carroll. referring to an act of chaos magick in the Now, which seemingly creates ripples into the past. Google "retroactive enchantment" or see Carroll's book, _Liber Kaos_.

SEE or SEEING - To "see" is the act of viewing the world (or anything within the world) according to its true nature, without the illusions and expectations we place onto the world through our own human programs. Seeing is more than looking. It is the seeker's greatest asset and tool in being able to recognize the illusory nature of the consensual reality (overlay) in which we all exist, often without ever realizing it.

SEVENTH SENSE – a perceptual plateau comprised of a combination of the 5 ordinary senses plus the "sixth sense" of psychic awareness or, more precisely, self-awareness. The author of immortalis-animus coined the term "the seventh sense" to describe the state we are aspiring to inhabit through this evolution of consciousness – for it is a state of being every bit as real and inhabitable as our world of ordinary awareness, but accessed with a more evolved set of preceptors which could be described as consciousness itself. The seventh sense is our world, but it is an expanded world. It is the world of the immortal, comprised of energy which is, by definition, indestructible and eternal.

SINGULARITY OF CONSCIOUSNESS – The self made Whole, the evolution of consciousness which results in a cohesive field of awareness existing ubiquitously and non-locally, infinitely and eternally. The immortal condition. The cohesive, fully integrated I-Am consisting of all components of the mortal self and the eternal double, brought together under a single assemblage point. The individuated totality of oneself.

SKINWALKER - A being who has the ability to temporarily inhabit the body of another. Real vampyres or any being in an immortal condition would possess the ability.

SORCERY: _1) The intuitive practice of magick. 2) A system of knowledge with specific practices, such as Wicca or Druidic magick._ I In essence, sorcery is a broad term used to encompass all magickal practices, whether learned or intuited.

SPIRIT – If earth, air, fire and water are the 4 natural elements, Spirit is the 5th element of creation. The living force or anima of the universe – impersonal, not a deity or entity; the living breath of power; the cohesive element of the all. In more modern language: spirit is "the force." There is no dark or light side of spirit. There is only spirit. How one uses it determines its manifestation.

SPONTANEOUS PARTHENOGENESIS – the act of something coming into existence out of the nothing, with no apparent cause. It is theorized by the author that the universe created itself from the void through an act of spontaneous parthenogenesis – a thought which wills itself into existence by saying I-Am. Furthermore, it could be visualized that the act of transmogrification is closely related to an act of spontaneous parthenogenesis - i.e., a willful creation.

TOTALITY: The sum total of one's life experience - including but not limited to the mortal self, the higher self, the immortal twin, and all other aspects of the self which extend through the quantum universe - outside of time. The totality of oneself would include seamless access to all memories of so-called past lives, parallel lives, and so on, gathered into a cohesive framework of awareness or singularity of consciousness. This is the immortal condition - the ability to open one's eyes inside the immortal twin, with flawless recall of one's total life experience.

TRANSMOGRIFICATION: As used throughout this book, transmogrification is an Intentional transference of all life energy (consciousness, awareness, individuated memory) from its mortal human coil into its immortal energy body. Because the energy body is a quantum state, it may take any form the seeker Intends, and may change form at will, depending on the skill & experience of the transmogrified individual. Transmogrification is the process through which the mortal seeker attains the immortal condition. Transmogrification is generally a long-term process, often requiring years of intent, meditation, and learning to glean energy directly from the multiverse.

TULPA: A thoughtform which may become real. Tulpas are usually born of extreme desire/need/imagination (such as a child's invisible friend), and may or may not take on a life of their own, depending on whether their creator nurtures them or neglects them. It may be argued that the vampyre twin begins as a tulpa and is made/Dreamed whole by the mortal self.

VAMPYRELAND: *1. A state of mind but also a state of being. 2. A separate reality which exists as a result of the seeker's own intent and will. 3. A quantum other-world or alternate dimensional reality.* Vampyreland is a concept which must be sensed, felt and intuited so that it is created with sufficient strength to exist both as a concept and as a separate reality capable of being inhabited. The master vampyre may exist simultaneously in the dayshine world and in vampyreland. This is the nature of vampyre duality - bi-location of mind/body/spirit. Vampyreland lies at the heart of the night that never ends - the state of mind which opens the door to all other-dimensional perceptions

WEB OF NON-LOCAL INFORMATION: The universe is comprised of energy, and at a quantum level, energy may be observed as "non-local" – meaning it is not confined to a single physical location. The web of non-local information refers to the fact that the seeker may glean information & knowledge directly from the fabric of the multiverse, where all knowledge exists in its raw form.

WILL - Will is the force which manifests want or need into reality. Will differs from intent. A simple analogy: intent is a true and genuine plan to visit the Grand Canyon. Will is the force that puts you behind the wheel of the car and drives. Will could also be described as the secret ingredient of sorcery, elusive as the wind and just as impossible to define.

(THE) WORK: The process of becoming immortal – the shedding of the programs and belief systems which stand between the mortal self and the immortal other. The Work may take many forms, and will not be the same for any two individuals. It is the work of becoming Whole.

Tonight is a haiku in ebony ink,
tomorrow a dalliance beyond the clock.
I walk between the shadows,
immortal talisman
cast in the shape of man.

ABOUT THE AUTHOR...
Mikal Nyght

Who I am isn't important. What I can show you through *Teachings of the Immortals* and *Darker Teachings of the Immortals* can save your life... *forever*.

As Goethe said... "Life is the childhood of our immortality." But because the human race has created and imprisoned itself in the matrix of so many false belief systems, most people willingly accept that death and mortality are simply part of the equation - but I am here to tell you that those beliefs are just as erroneous as the belief that the earth is flat or that the stars are lights shining through from heaven.

The higher truth is that you are the most powerful being in the universe - and the only thing standing between you and your rightful immortality is the belief that keeps insisting you are mortal. The higher truth is that you can be anything you want to be because all components of your mind/body/spirit are comprised of infinite energy... and energy is already "immortal" by its very nature. Energy can neither be created nor destroyed - it can only change form.

What this means to *you* is that you are not the spiritually-impotent organic creature most religions and governments would have you believe. You have at your fingertips the power of all creation - *literally*! You have the power to transform yourself from organic to inorganic, from human to super-human, from mortal to immortal. And it all begins with a thought.

All things exist within the realm of possibility, but only some things will be forced to go through the motions of actually occurring. The knowledge I have gathered over a lifetime (and more) is now available to you through my books, my website and my free online forum, Immortal Spirit. Remember: you can be anything you want to be. The only limitations are those you bring with you.

This is your life. Live well and live forever!

Mikal Nyght

SONS OF NEVERLAND
An Erotic Novel by Della Van Hise

...if you enjoyed Anne Rice's *Vampire Chronicles*, you will surely love *Sons of Neverland* for its bold depiction of love, sex and death: the three most profound experiences every human being must face. *Sons of Neverland* takes the vampire mythos out of Hollywood and brings to it a gritty realism mixed with some of the most erotic and sensuous writing in the genre. This is one I'll read again for the dark philosophical look at immortality, as well as the resplendent and emotionally mature love story...
-Print Review, North County Sentinel

The virtuosity shown here is only the beginning of a pyrotechnic talent unfolding into the hidden dimensions of the human and nonhuman spirit.
-Jacqueline Lichtenberg, Author of Sime/Gen series

From the Back Cover

"I know you're afraid, Stefan," he told me, resting a steady hand on my shoulder. "So we'll speak with reverence of your death for a moment and then we'll simply do it. I think it would be best that way, without so much angst and contemplation, yes?"

It was so easy for him, so natural to seduce a mortal soul right out of the vessel that held it. My heart pounded, wild drums. My tears fell, a fatal storm. I couldn't speak, and so he took my silence as surrender. His fingers caressed my throat, luring the blood to the surface.

"Now let the world be gone," he whispered. "Let the world go away so the night can come in." And with that, he seized me with his teeth in a grip so fierce I felt the cramp of torment all the way through to my feet. My eyes flashed open, but I clamped them tightly shut, afraid I would see Death in the room. Warmth poured down my neck, a rushing red river caught by the devil's lips...

**Available at www.eyescrypublications.com or
order from your local bookseller**

Quantum Shaman: Diary of a Nagual Woman
by Della Van Hise

Diary of a Nagual Woman is the compelling true story of one woman's journey on the path with heart. A personal and chilling confrontation with the very nature of life and death, which brings the reader face to face with the shaman's double: the immortal & mysterious Other who takes on a life of his own, & manifests the key to unlocking our own evolution of consciousness. The double is the higher self, the energy body, the dreaming body, but contrary to what we have been led to believe, the higher self is not necessarily confined to energy alone, as the author discovered on an otherwise insignificant morning in the spring of 1988.

In this book, you will meet Orlando at the same time the author first encounters him - and it is a meeting that is both humorous and life-altering, for it brings what is traditionally considered impossible into the realm of possibility, and launches both author and reader into a journey that has no beginning and no end - and is as personal to every seeker as his or her own fingerprints. For anyone familiar with the works of Carlos Castaneda, *Diary of a Nagual Woman* continues the journey and expands into areas seldom explored in other works, bringing a quantum comprehension to what has traditionally been considered a mystical path alone.

An excellent companion-book to *Teachings of the Immortals.*

www.quantumshaman.com

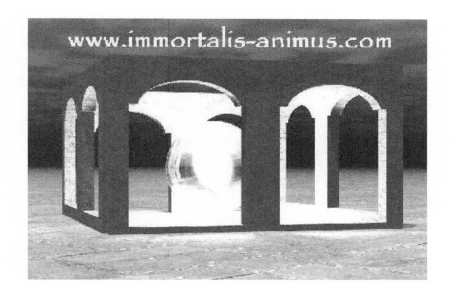

You have to __be__ immortal
before you will know how to __become__ immortal.

Made in the USA
Las Vegas, NV
17 May 2024